Susan Chan.

Effervescence

A True-Life Tale of Autism and of Courage

"She was not perseverating; she was watching, learning and growing. *She was working and she was only four years old!* I do believe that she had a plan and that much of the reason that she was now lashing out at the world less frequently and with less intensity, was because she felt loved and accepted. She knew that her uniqueness was embraced. She was then able to channel much of that explosive energy more positively, into self exploration and "human nature" exploration. *I believe to the depth of my soul, that the greatest gift and the single, most significant form of therapy she has ever received, has been acceptance, of letting her see and feel that our goal was not to force a square peg into a round hole*".

Further Praise of

Effervescence

"I loved this book! In spite of having family staying with us, I couldn't wait to keep reading *Effervescence* and finished it in just three days. I have learned so much about autism that I wasn't aware of before. I feel that this book should be read by all parents, not just those who can relate to autism. Ms. Brenneman's writing was so much from the heart, it gave me goose bumps!" *Eileen Duncan, primary school teacher.*

"I have read many books on my own journey to understand my eldest daughter. I have read parenting books, medical books, educational books, self-help books and books about raising children with many different challenges. *Effervescence* is the first book that I have read that is a personal account of the experiences of both a child and parents working together. Our daughters are very different and yet I see similarities as well.

This story is about a child who has both struggled and succeeded. Although I have the support of many wonderful friends and family, at times it still feels like a lonely journey. This book made me feel less alone.

I plan to read *Effervescence* to my daughters one day. I also look forward to reading *The Castle We Called Home.* *Lillian Lambert, parent.*

$\mathcal{U}$pon reading *Effervescence* and *The Castle We Called Home*
(the original short tales), November 2003

"Dear Nolan and Simone,

What a tribute to your combined creativity and intelligence that you
were able to enter heads filled with soft, pink, zebra-striped realms or
solid, castle walls. To give 150% of yourselves and to see the sweetness
and beauty that others, particularly "professionals" weren't always able
to see, is a God-given gift.

Once I began reading, I could not put them down until I finished. I
truly believe Simone that you should be seeking a publisher, since you
say you have many diaries and obviously many stories waiting to be told.
Your stories need to be shared, not only with educators and professional
medical people, but also with the general public who can be so ignorant
and unforgiving.

I always had a costume box in my classroom for impromptu performances.
To have a whole drama-costume room in your home is phenomenal!
The "effervescence" of love sparkles through all the pages of your tales
and is such a testimony to your inner strengths as a family. Simone,
you have obviously found your calling as a natural teacher and in
my opinion, a director, games creator, costume designer, art therapist,
counselor and behaviorist". *Judy Williams, high school teacher*

Effervescence

A True-Life Tale of Autism and of Courage

Simone Brenneman

authorHOUSE®

AuthorHouse™
1663 Liberty Drive
Bloomington, IN 47403
www.authorhouse.com
Phone: 1-800-839-8640

To provide anonymity, most of the names in this book are fictional.

First published by AuthorHouse   7/16/2009

ISBN: 978-1-4389-7754-6 (sc)
ISBN: 978-1-4389-7753-9 (hc)

Library of Congress Control Number: 2009905945

Printed in the United States of America
Bloomington, Indiana

This book is printed on acid-free paper.

Author's Website:
effervescentclarity.com

To

The Moody Blues

Justin Hayward   John Lodge   Graeme Edge
Ray Thomas   Mike Pinder

And to Karyn
I will always blow you kisses.

Forward

Only one letter separates autistic from artistic – a typo I've corrected more than once. But what happens when an artistic parent has an autistic child, and then another very different autistic child? The answer lies in this fascinating book by Simone Brenneman. On one level, her story is the story of many families with autistic children. It is a story of love and loss, of unceasing work and dedication, of complications and adaptations. On another level, this is a story unique to Genevieve and Hayden, their siblings and family. It is a life that only an artist could live and a story that only an artist could tell.

Ms. Brenneman uses her gifts of sensitivity and creativity to enter deeply into the unique worlds of her autistic children, to truly understand them and to see the world through their eyes. She uses her gifts of the language and imagery to allow us the privilege of visiting these worlds with her. Genevieve and Hayden have both thrived with their mother's ability to enter their worlds well enough to feel understood and valued. She has guided them forward not by pushing and pulling but, like a fairy, skipping down the path ahead of them, weaving stories and images so well that her children often followed. She has been able to translate our "mysterious" world to her children and, when necessary, translate her mysterious children to our world. In this wonderful book Ms. Brenneman goes beyond translation and becomes our guide through the fascinating world of autism and the heart-warming journey of her family.

Dr. Glen Davies, Ph.D.,R.Psych.
Director, ABLE Developmental Clinic Inc.
British Columbia, Canada

Author's Note

The biggest challenge in creating this book was conceptualizing how I could tell the story of two complex children with autism, and their family, in a way that would not have the head spinning of anyone who chose to pick it up to read. The complexities, the bizarre, the heartfelt, the heart-wrenching, the amazing and the lovely: they all happened. They fill the dozens of journals and thousands of pages of notes and documents that I've saved along the way. It's all there.

Initially this book was written as two separate stories, two tales, presented within the confines of one book cover. But there was too much! Your head would have been spinning ridiculously by the time you got to the second tale. Not only that, each child has been affected by autism so uniquely that each deserves a cover of her and his own. Genevieve deserves to have her story presented and published first, not remotely because she was born before her brother Hayden; but for a very specific reason: though every aspect of her life has been touched by the fact that she has autism, her story, her needs and her challenges have often been overshadowed by his intensely complex and often aggressive presence. Too frequently therapists' time and resources that should have been allocated to her were directed at him, because it would have been pointless to put out little fires with her when the blazing inferno that was Hayden, surrounded her. Often she had to retreat to her world of autism to survive and to escape living with him. As parents, sometimes we had to let her go there because we knew that at least she would be safe, and much of the time, happy.

Genevieve did survive and she most certainly did thrive. She has captivated her family and the world around her. It only makes sense that her story should be told separately and that it should be told first. It's her chance to shine and to reveal pieces of her world and her unique and inspirational journey. I hope that her story, her tale as I have presented it, will also whet your appetite and entice you to seek out the second tale, *The Castle We Called Home*. It tells of an even more complex journey filled with the intricate webbing of the pervasive and fascinating impact of autism on our family.

Midway through writing this book, a therapist asked me if I was planning to include charts and diagrams and checklists, "do's and don'ts" so to speak, to offer bits of insight into the world of autism. That was when I realized that somewhere since this book's conception I had made a conscious decision *not* to follow that format. That is the whole point in writing this book and in sharing my family's experiences.

So many people connected to this field seem to be searching for that "perfect book", the one that will have all the answers to autism neatly categorized in easy steps, for families, caregivers and therapists to follow. I've had parents of newly-diagnosed children call me; I've had caregivers call me, asking if I can just give them the name of the book that I found that laid it all out, that wrapped it up in one nice, little package. That book doesn't exist. That *is* the point. And if you are looking for it, you are missing the point and you are also missing much of what is most fascinating about autism.

There are many books that can give you insight into autism from a more scientific and therapeutic vantage point than I can give; and they do it well. I can't begin to offer that kind of expertise and it has never been my intention or my desire. My dream has been to let you take a peek inside the very complex world that has been my home for a long time. My way is not to provide outlines and checklists but to paint pictures, pictures that can enable you to see and feel autism, to let it permeate through you. One of my driving desires and my prevailing philosophy really, is to ask anyone who is connected to someone with autism, to look beyond what is right in front of you. Stand back and watch and listen and *feel* them and their world. Live in their world and learn from them. As much as I think I have had the opportunity to teach my children, it is barely a fraction of what I have learned from them.

I can't honestly say that there has been a single day in the past eighteen years that was an "easy" day and certainly not a typical day, by most family's standards; but every single day my eyes have been opened to things I would never have otherwise known or understood. It has been a journey! Our path may not fit for all; it can't possibly because every person with autism is affected so uniquely, but it fit for us and it has made each of us who we are today. We are very blessed.

Effervescence and *The Castle We Called Home* are not only tales about autism; they are tales about courage and about evolving.

Chapter 1

Imagine a beautiful little girl, with long curly, wild red hair, spinning in circles, completely delighted by all that she feels! She wears a long, blue dress, a replica of the one Cinderella wore to the ball. As you watch her, you get the sense that she isn't dreaming of Cinderella; in her heart and in her body, she *is* Cinderella.

Now picture the same little girl, lying on her tummy, spinning on a merry-go-round, dipping her beautiful, long red hair in the puddle of mud that encircles the merry-go-round. When it comes to a stop, she savors the wonderful sensation of the cold mud running down her face. She then submerges her entire body in the puddle, as happy as can be and entirely oblivious to the stares of the people around her.

Now picture that same little girl, in her comfortable home, surrounded by a family who love and adore her. Her mom asks a simple question, like: "Sweetie, what kind of cereal would you like?" Instantly, her beautiful face is filled with intense emotion and she screams, more like a wild animal than a child, for five minutes, or it may continue for two hours. The only thing that might interrupt the screaming is her stopping, occasionally, to frantically bite her wrist, hard enough to leave teeth marks.

Would it surprise you to learn that I have just described a high-functioning autistic child?

Now take a peak at the same child at age twelve, entering her classroom each day. Her teacher marvels to herself, as she watches this young girl navigate skillfully, smoothly and seemingly naturally throughout the classroom. Had the teacher not known her student's history of autism, she likely would never have guessed. In her own words, the only time this teacher is aware of the child's autism, is when she reads the amazing stories and illustrations created by this extraordinary girl. She would then muse to herself: "There is no way a "typical" grade-seven student could write and draw like this!"

Do you get the feeling that an amazing transformation has taken place? Is the child no longer autistic? Has she grown out of it? Has she learned through behavior management to "manage" it? Was she just "a little bit autistic" and now she's "better?" There is no simple answer; autism is far too complex and diverse a disorder for it to be addressed so simply. But it is a fascinating disorder and this child's life has been an incredible journey! Her name is Genevieve.

Chapter 2

All children are life's greatest blessing; but some children touch the world around them in ways that are truly unique and profound. Genevieve is one of those and there is much to be learned from her. Terms like "effervescent" and "her feet never quite touch the ground" describe her best. To know Genevieve is to genuinely know the meaning of determination, humor and sparkle. To know Genevieve, is to see life, if only in glimpses, through a most unique and fascinating perspective: through the eyes of autism.

To do so, you will need to sit back, relax and shift gears. Recapture the image of the merry-go-round, the mud, the red curls, the screaming, the navigating…this tale will take you through an eighteen-year journey, a journey that is still very much in progress. It is my pleasure, but most of all, my honor and my privilege to be your guide and the author of this tale. As her mom, I became her "stepping stone", the bridge from "her world" to ours and the person she was able to trust first and foremost. It is with Genevieve's approval and her fascination in learning about herself, joined with her desire to open the eyes of the world around her about autism, that I tell her story.

I can't imagine anyone in the world being more blessed than I. I open up my heart to you now and hope that you will share my fascination and immense respect for all children and adults who share the common threads of autism.

To begin an exploration of the life of an autistic child, and the impact on his or her family, you do need to be equipped with a little of the technical background. My intention is not to provide a comprehensive description but more to offer words and images, to enable you to feel what autism is, at least as it is in our family and in our experiences. I will simply say that autism is a developmental disorder with much speculation and uncertainty as to the specific causes. However, it is known that there is a defect in the body's system that processes incoming sensory information, which in turn, causes the autistic individual to over-react to certain stimuli and under-react to others. To block out the bombardment of incoming stimulation, the individual then withdraws from his or her environment. If he or she chooses, or is thereby forced to withdraw into his or her own world, even sudden, loud noises may not startle them. It is very confusing to those around them and the reason why hearing impairment is often the first issue questioned by family and doctors. Most autistic individuals are extremely sensitive to noises, colors, lights and scents; yet they seem rather "disconnected" from their bodies and certainly their emotions.

Tactile stimulation is of extreme importance to autistic individuals, especially children. All children need tactile stimulation, but autistic children need much more. For most, this need moves to the point of obsession, because that is where they gain a sense of security and control, and how they learn. As autistic children do not take in information and process it in the "normal" way, they do not learn by "osmosis" the way most children typically do. This is particularly true with respect to them understanding emotions and behaviors, both their own and of the people around them. Donna Williams, an adult and author with autism, described this issue in her amazing book *Nobody Nowhere*, by writing: "On the whole, they get through life by rote, learning rules for dealing with situations but often having very little understanding of the meaning and significance of what they are dealing with. They also find it hard to process information about people and their relationships. This can vary from an inability to recognize facial expressions or even know which part of the face tells us what someone is feeling, to a general difficulty in understanding what is going on in common social situations, and in recognizing what someone is feeling from their tone of voice, choice of words, and other cues in normal conversation" [1].

The impact of an autistic individual's struggle to function socially, is enormous and probably the most well known and complex challenge. I have come to refer to it as "social strings attached" and it underlies the feeling that for someone with autism, their lives are an ongoing struggle to keep the world out, juxtaposed by the struggle and desire to join it. Has this struggle been a significant one in my daughter Genevieve's life? Absolutely; it has been from the very beginning and each and every day since.

Chapter 3

Being a tale, this story probably should have started with: "Once upon a time…" How did our tale begin? Did we suspect that something about our daughter was different? Over the years, countless people have asked me that question, many of them people I had never even met before, like it was some common ground that everyone had a right to know. As parents, we've been poked and prodded; Genevieve and her siblings have been poked and prodded, because we are a unique bunch. To me, the images of our early years are very clear. I remember them all vibrantly. And for what I don't remember, I have a stack of journals, and thousands of pages of documentation, each bursting with depictions, facts and speculations to jog my memory.

Like many autistic children, Genevieve appeared to be "normal" for the first part of her life. I wouldn't say she was "typical" because she had a placid, captivating calmness and sweetness that was very unique. We saw it from the moment she was born and we interpreted it more as something wondrous and lovely, not something that was worrisome. We still do. Of course, now that as parents we are well versed in the language of autism, we can look back and immediately see many clues; but at the time, how could we have known what they meant? We were so in love with this incredibly happy and content baby, with her red, curly hair and her perfect rosebud lips. But as the mysteries of autism began to unfold, a little bit later in her life, many pieces from her little past fell into place.

Even before birth, I sensed there was something really unique about Genevieve and I commented frequently to friends and family, and wrote about it often in my journal. She was my third pregnancy in three years, so I was very in tune with my body and my babies. But there was something in the way that she moved within me, and how and when she moved, that felt very different. She seemed uniquely playful, yet at the same time, like someone who just couldn't stay comfortable in her surroundings. I knew she was going to be a real character, with a unique personality. That I could feel.

It doesn't surprise me that even today as a teenager, Genevieve loves to squirm and wrap her legs and feet around me, or slip her hand in mine, only to pull it away and then slip it back, as if there's confusion in her mind as to whether or not it is an enjoyable experience.

As an infant, Genevieve was exceptionally calm and content. To some extent, Nolan (her dad) and I patted ourselves and each other on the back, attributing it to our parenting skills and the playful, happy home we had created. At that time, we had a lovely home, not only with Genevieve, but with her sister Sydney, who at the time of Genevieve's birth was three, and Kobe our son, who was fifteen months. I think in our defense, we did deserve much of the credit. And for me, I was in my element; this was my dream come true and I saw every day as an adventure. What could life possibly hold that could be more fun and rewarding than this?

But as I look back now, with years of accumulated knowledge and insight, I see that a big part of Genevieve's complacent behavior was the second piece of the autism puzzle.

In her first year, Genevieve hardly ever cried and desired very little attention. Though she enjoyed being with her family, she was equally happy being on her own. She slept and ate well and met the usual baby milestones, such as sitting, crawling, standing and walking. If anything, she reached them a little early because she had the ultimate incentive of wanting to keep up with her treasured siblings.

As a baby, Genevieve was very social and would brighten up when we entered the room. She loved Sydney and Kobe and the three of them were like a litter of puppies. Often I'd find her hidden under the patio table, conspiring with Kobe, both of them munching on Cheesies, or lying together, each enjoying their soothers and probably contemplating the true meaning of life, or at least, whatever adventure they might next share.

Often, both Sydney and Kobe would hop in Genevieve's crib with her. She loved to snuggle up close; yet she equally loved to be on her own. We have many photos of the three of them, arms and little bodies wrapped around each other. But many times, she would run off to seek time on her own. Though it was convenient, with three small children, to have one so content to be on her own, the sense that this was an unnatural isolation sometimes nagged away at me.

Genevieve loved people and seemed fascinated by a certain amount of chaos. For her first birthday, we had a "Three Little Pigs" party with lots of family and friends. All the kids pranced around in the piggy ears and noses that we had made; Genevieve was captivated by the people, the presents, the attention and the chocolate cake. There was something in her that felt a bit "different", but she was happy and saw the world with wonder, as any one year old should.

One question people have often asked me about is "eye contact". Did Genevieve make eye contact? Of course she did, and lots of it. But it was, at times, "different". She loved to stare intently into our eyes, so much so that Nolan and I often commented that she appeared to be more interested in watching her own reflection than in connecting with us. We never would have dreamed that that characteristic was one of the most marked indicators of autism. What stood out the very most about Genevieve was that she had fierce determination and was very active. There was a certain energy and sparkle about her that was absolutely captivating and uniquely "Genevieve".

As she neared the eighteen month mark, a transformation began to take place in her and in our family. Everything in our home and our lives began to change drastically. Life was turned upside down and twisted around, as her complacent behavior was literally transformed. It was gradual at first, and then snowballed rapidly, making us five people living a nightmarish existence. We desperately tried to figure out why!

For one, Genevieve's lack of speech concerned us. It wasn't that she couldn't speak; it was more that she wasn't "conversational". She was sweet and affectionate and loved to gaze into our eyes, but it felt like she was looking through us, like she was more interested and more comfortable watching her own reflection, than in connecting with us. And she clearly cherished time spent on her own, particularly in the safe haven of her crib.

Genevieve had absolutely no instinctive sense of danger and was drawn to climb high, or lie at the very edge of a high landing, looking down. She would dash off in any and every direction with no apparent need, desire or understanding about staying close to her family. At that point, I tied bells to her shoes to assist me when we were out. Though she was very bright and picked things up quickly, she seemed oblivious to much.

More significant than Genevieve's increased need and desire for solitude, was her incredibly volatile behavior. She exasperated us and the world around her, with unbelievably intense and frequent temper tantrums. It was like someone had flicked a switch, completely altering her personality, her nature and her temperament. The issue of pain tolerance was mystifying as well. She seemed practically unaware and unaffected by the pain of teething, as if she simply didn't feel physical pain. Her new baby teeth just seemed to appear.

Chapter 4

What saved our sanity was the fact that when Genevieve was calm and happy, she was captivating! She truly was a unique soul and she continued to turn heads with her wild red hair, her chubby cheeks, her sweetness and her absolute effervescence. When she walked, she giggled, like life was the funniest thing. She appeared to experience life on a whole different level than the rest of us.

By age two, Genevieve could speak, but development seemed to come practically to a standstill, as she clearly lacked the ability and inclination for conversational speech. Increasingly, eye contact was something she avoided; it seemed almost painful to her, particularly with people outside of her immediate family. She now appeared to be totally oblivious to pain and coldness. It was absolutely impossible to keep a jacket on her, even when walking in the snow. It seemed as if wearing it tormented her skin and her entire being.

Yet by contrast, she loved being naked and wrapped up in snugly blankets. Sensations like being submerged in cold mud were delectable. She loved to snuggle in our big, queen-sized bed, with her bottle and her Sydney and Kobe, but only briefly. Then she'd toddle off to the safety of her own bed and her isolation. At times she would revel in the pleasure of snuggling on the couch with us, to watch a movie and munch on popcorn; but it would be short-lived, and she'd leave. She enjoyed her routine morning bottle and snuggle time with me; but for the most part, she would deflect our offers to sit and snuggle and would always run off down the hallway to our bed or to her own, to enjoy her own company.

More and more, she existed alongside us, but not really with us.

Genevieve had an absolute insistence on wearing long, ruffled princess dresses. Shrieking and sobbing would result if she was forced to wear anything else. It literally wrenched her heart, to the very depth of her soul! Clearly there was an element of fantasy, like an actor in a costume; and it was evident that there was no point in forcing the issue of wearing other clothes.

Genevieve's sense of hearing had us mystified. At times, we were certain she had developed a serious hearing impairment. We'd call and call and she wouldn't respond or even flinch. It was like she either didn't hear us or she didn't have a clue about the concept of responding. By contrast, often we'd whisper, in what should have been literally out of her range of hearing, and she would hear it perfectly. She was clearly bright and very intelligent, making it all very curious and most discerning.

Spinning in circles oddly filled a need in Genevieve, particularly in social settings. When playing with toys, much of her play was incredibly creative and imaginative; but she used toys in the most extraordinary, non-typical ways, like they appeared differently to her than they would have to other children. Her love of fantasy was becoming an intricate part of her personality and her interpretation of life.

Yet, ironically, much of Genevieve's play was exceptionally organized and non-creative. She'd spend hours lining up and categorizing dozens of small animal figurines. From a very early age, it was obvious that these inanimate objects were as real and as meaningful and precious to her as any person in her life. By watching her and how she played and interacted with her beloved animal figurines, I could see that at least part of the appeal they held for her was that they did not have the same "social strings attached" that real people or even dolls had.

In our bathroom, we had a very long counter with an equally long mirror above it. Genevieve would sit on the counter, literally for hours, dressed in a princess dress and a crown, lining up animal toys. The little girl in the mirror staring back at her (who truly was, in Genevieve's mind a princess), was the playmate she sought out the most and felt most at peace with. And between herself and her reflected "playmate", they had twice the number of animal friends!

At times, like in the bathroom with her private world of animal friends, Genevieve was the perfect picture of serenity. Yet the screaming and the volatile, unexplainable behaviors in the outside world only worsened. They couldn't have been a more marked contradiction to the angelic girl we saw in the bathroom mirror when we peeked in!

Chapter 5

CReading about Genevieve's first two years must be very confusing; it was confusing to us. By now, life with her was incredibly volatile and the littlest thing could set her off. We were living with a time bomb, constantly bracing ourselves, for the next time it would go off. We'd just get through one incident, with barely enough time to pull ourselves back together, before we'd be hit by another. She would scream, stomp, flop herself on the floor and frequently hit her head. She would kick and sometimes bite her own wrist, leaving teeth marks. Sometimes she'd bite us.

It was hard to know what to do. Reprimanding her only made things worse. Sometimes we would just let her outbursts run their course; sometimes we'd hold her as tightly as we could to prevent her from hurting herself and to hopefully, at least make her feel loved. As a family, we were exhausted, drained and yet completely mystified. So often, she was happy and carefree. Her sparkling personality, her intelligence and aptitude for learning and understanding things kept us filled more with wonder than concern.

But by age two and a half, Nolan and I were worried, damn worried. It wasn't just the screaming and the horrendously volatile behavior and the fact that it was worsening; it was now the speech issue. Speech had taken on a new level of mystery and concern, as not only was Genevieve's vocabulary and ability to speak not developing, it was diminishing. She was using fewer words and often resisted our attempts to converse. She seemed innately uncomfortable with the concept of speech. And our concerns went even deeper: Genevieve had become a red-haired beauty who frolicked through life, sometimes in our world, but most times in her own world, very much in isolation.

For me, the feeling that I was neglecting my child was unbearable. I was so willing and able to give her tons of time and attention, yet she was off in her own little world so much of the time. I found myself actually having to make a point of initiating contact with her. I literally had to remind myself to try to include her when Sydney, Kobe and I were playing. It was like we would actually forget about her. Equally bizarre, was Sydney and Kobe's evolving relationship with Genevieve. They loved her and adored her; they were, in fact, fascinated by her and her free spirit and her unique take on the world. Yet she slipped in and out of their world so frequently that they often forgot about her. And that was when she was calm and playful. Much of the time, she was wild, volatile and impossible to live with.

I can hardly put into words how bizarre it was. How could you forget about your child, especially a toddler? How could siblings forget about their sister? But that was where things were with Genevieve. That was how truly separate from us she kept herself, so much of the time. I really, really scared myself when I realized how much she was isolating herself and that we were literally forgetting about her. I almost can't believe I'm putting it in black and white for people to read.

I remember with absolute clarity where we were and what we were doing, when my whole world stopped moving, when my heart sank to my toes and the words: "We're loosing her!" lanced through my brain. Those words were all I could see and all I could hear. They changed my world forever.

That moment came when Genevieve was two and a half, and we were at my sister's house. There was Genevieve, frolicking through Charlize's home, a beautiful little girl with a captivating aura, who was so trapped in her own little world. We'd watched the transformation in her behavior for a year: the incredibly intense temper tantrums and her need to be alone. Yet at times she was still so effervescent, so extraordinarily calm and sparkly. But that day there was just something so painfully clear in seeing Sydney and Kobe in happy play with their three cousins, juxtaposed with their baby sister who was happy but deeply trapped and lost in a different world.

At that moment, everything made sense; it all pulled together. Feelings I hadn't been able to pull together before, or to articulate, suddenly found a voice in my head and my heart. The complexity of the situation became so clear, and I saw that for such a long time, Genevieve had *wanted* to be a part of us, but she existed alongside of us, because she didn't know *how* to be a part of us. I think she wanted it desperately but pulled back because it was overwhelming to her. She didn't have the tools to make it happen. For me, thoughts and feelings I'd been struggling with for months suddenly, in a matter of seconds, all pulled together and became so clear. I said over and over, frantically in my mind: "We're loosing her!"

Charlize's home is a beautiful house, tucked away amongst tall fir trees, creeks and ravines, and very near mountains. It's a little bit dark, because of all the trees, but it is rich, green and beautiful. Maybe it wasn't just seeing the other five children interact that made my revelation happen. Maybe, in part, it was also the setting that allowed it to all come clear to me; it made it safe and visual enough for me to see the reality of how serious the situation with Genevieve was.

It was a big house, with several split levels and rooms that went off in all different directions. The house was representative of how I saw Genevieve at that moment, at that time in her life: she was a beautiful creature, happy but trapped, and confined by all of those different walls, those different rooms. Though some of those walls and some of the rooms were considered by her to be safe, they were walls and rooms nonetheless.

At that moment, in my sister's home, I vowed to Genevieve that I was going to turn things around for her, that I was not going to loose her. I was going to find a way to open up all those little rooms in her mind that she retreated to. I vowed to figure out where she went and more importantly, *why* she needed to go there. I didn't know what the problem was, or how I was going to do it; but I knew absolutely that I would find a way. Of that I had complete faith.

I knew I had to keep her close to my heart, desperately close, and that I had to turn my life upside down and get into her world. I knew that I'd have to do whatever it took to see the world through her eyes. I could feel that she was in another place, maybe not all of the time, but at that point, most of the time. I had to find out why she wanted and needed to be there. I needed her to take me there, because I was not going to lose her!

Chapter 6

On those moments, in my sister's house, I was able to grasp all the little, nagging suspicions and concerns that had been growing in my mind for months. My head and my heart were in sync, willing and able to grasp the severity of the transformation that had been altering my child and my family. And I was bursting with sheer determination!

I had no doubt that I was embarking on a journey and that it had to be a personal journey, as well as a family one. I sensed it was huge but probably through luck, had no comprehension or inkling just how complex and pervasive it would end up being.

"Perspective"; it was a matter of perspective. Little of Genevieve's past year had made any sense, so I stood back, took in a huge breathe and said to myself: "Who was Genevieve as an infant and who is she now?" I focused all of my energy on that thought, on those comparative images. I made my mind replay all of the comments from well-meaning friends and family like: "She'll grow out of it". "It's the Terrible Two's". "It's because she's the third". Why had those comments infuriated me for so many months? I realized it was because they were meaningless in the context of who Genevieve had become. In retrospect, maybe a scattered few, like my sister Charlize, were brave and intuitive enough to see that there was something seriously wrong, but they just didn't know how to broach such a delicate matter. But I felt that most people either had their eyes closed or preferred to see it as simply Genevieve's personality. One woman close to our family had seemed so proud of herself, like she'd discovered the answer to the mystery, when she stated: "Genevieve just doesn't *want* to talk!" She acted like it was a child's god-forsaken right not to talk, if she was just too stubborn or too lazy. Some said that Genevieve wasn't talking because "Sydney and Kobe were talking for her".

For God's sake, did these people have their eyes closed? Anyone who took the time to watch and listen would have seen that at that point, Sydney and Kobe never talked for their sister; most of the time they practically forgot about her. Even when she was in their presence, she wasn't really "with them". And this was not just a speech issue. There were the bizarre and volatile behaviors. Could they not see that even though she appeared happy some of the time, frolicking in her own little princess world, she desperately wanted to be a part of her family; but she genuinely didn't know how!

I racked my brain, questioning: Why would she have an extensive vocabulary, albeit not conversational, and then loose so much of it? What mystified and tormented me the most about Genevieve, was the screaming and the horrendous temper tantrums. It simply didn't make any sense. Why would an exceptionally calm and placid baby now spend vast amounts of time each day, screaming like a wild, caged animal? If one more person attributed her behaviors to the "Terrible Twos", or any of those other usual anecdotes, I thought I would scream and tantrum myself.

Everything kept coming back to the same realization: this was not our Genevieve. And it had nothing to do with personality, stubbornness, age, or birth order!

And so, I reached for the only tool I felt I could use: "Fantasy". I'd always been fascinated by the way Genevieve played and how she used toys in such unusual and unique ways. It was obvious that she saw things from a completely different perspective. And there was the very uncanny connection that she had with animal toys over people toys, particularly the Piggy dollhouse I had made for her days before she was born. The key had to be somewhere in there. And what about her insistence on wearing princess dresses? They had to be an integral part of this.

With my new-found conviction and motive, I watched her and listened to her more closely. I documented and pondered and contemplated. I did everything I could think of to see and feel the world, not only through her eyes but through her body and her senses. (A number of years later, long after Genevieve had been diagnosed with autism, I found a line in Temple Grandin's wonderful book *Emergence*, where Temple reflects upon a teacher who played a vital role in her life and consequently, in her own emergence. When I read it, it made my heart skip a beat, because I hoped it represented the approach that I had been so intent on using to reach Genevieve, at that critical time in her life. It read: "He didn't try to draw me into his world, but came, instead, into my world" [2].

Once I took that step with Genevieve, doors opened. I had always felt a strong bond between her and myself, despite her reclusive nature; that bond intensified and I can only describe it as one that brings tears to my eyes when I think of it. It truly felt like an actual physical, magnetic bond or force and it was very real; I can feel traces of it right now as I envision those early years working one on one with her. It was like there was a pulling and receiving force that I felt from just below my collarbone to my hips. It is very hard to put into words that will make sense, but I remember feeling it intensely and commenting on it many times in my journals. I knew it was real and that she felt it too. I think it was the energy of her soul and mine meeting, on levels that far exceeded words. She understood that I was unobtrusively and respectfully, tip-toeing into her world, on levels that I hadn't before, and she was drawing it in.

Our new journey had begun! If I was asked to put "my strategy, my concept, my vision" or whatever you might want to call it, into words, I would simply say: "Watch the Disney movie *Fantasia*". Essentially, that is who Genevieve and I became. In *Fantasia*, the illustrators magically matched symphonic musical pieces with characters that they created. Every flower, every drop of rain, every object was given a unique and distinct personality, as real and as vibrant as any human character could be. They all worked and interacted together in a most glorious and creative way. *That* was what our daily life became.

Ironically, at that point in my life, I had never seen the movie *Fantasia*. Years later, we discovered it and when I was watching it with my kids, I was taken aback, because I realized that it was the concept and the perspective I had so naturally taken with Genevieve. In other words, I hadn't taken the concept from seeing it appear onscreen; I *saw* the concept, by *watching* Genevieve and by "breathing her in". It then came bursting out of me. I could feel through every inch of my being that the personification of safe, non-human and therefore, non-intrusive characters, held the key.

I do believe that when we did discover the movie *Fantasia,* Genevieve too, if only on a subconscious level, made the connection about the significance it held for us both and as a family. To this day, she and I share a deep, inner glow whenever we hear references to the movie or see parts of it. There is a spoken and unspoken connection between us about it.

Our "Fantasia-like existence" was the way Genevieve and I worked together. We animated absolutely everything. For instance, instead of saying "Genevieve, where are your shoes?" or even worse, making a demand like: "Genevieve, go and get your shoes!" (which would have been received as intrusive, and therefore destined to be met with either shutdown or a screaming fit), I would personify things and say: "Shoes, where are you?" Genevieve immediately bought into it and connected deeply and innately.

At the time, I didn't really know why it worked; I was just so thrilled and relieved to see that it was, in fact, working! And it happened quickly. It was evident in the way Genevieve carried herself and how she began to respond to things. Though much of the volatile, erratic behavior continued, there was within her, a sense of peace and security emerging. She seemed more connected to the environment and to the people around her.

A genuine fascination was, in fact, emerging in Genevieve, and she welcomed these animated, everyday items, like her shoes, into her life. More of her amazing sparkle was shining through than we had seen in a very long time. What was of equal excitement was seeing that despite her young age, of two and a half, what I felt coming from her was gratitude! On some level, conscious or not, she understood that I was reaching out to her. I do believe with certainty that she understood that I was not asking her to change and jump into my world. She could see that it was quite the opposite. She felt my adoration and fascination for who she was, and she felt my hope and desire, that she would let me go there with her.

Two years later, at the very time that Genevieve would be diagnosed with autism, Donna Williams' book *Nobody Nowhere* appeared in bookstores. Two lines in her book made perfect sense to me when I read them, as they described who Genevieve was, back when we began our "process" and why the concept of personification was so immediately effective. They read: "If I liked something, I would try to loose myself in my fascination for it. Things, unlike people, were welcome to be a part of me" [3].

The rock group, *The Moody Blues*, my mentors and my single greatest source of inspiration throughout our autism journey, have a song called "Meet Me Halfway". That song and that concept have played in my head for many years; you could say it has become my autism anthem. It reinforces to me the importance and the power of stepping outside my world, and letting Genevieve (and my autistic son who was yet to be born), see that I saw her world, that I valued it and that I asked only that in return, she take a step, just a step, outside of hers. At that point,

Genevieve was far from meeting me halfway, but to a two and a half year old with tiny baby feet, her steps were pretty big steps indeed!

Nolan, Sydney and Kobe were quick studies and adapted immediately to our new, "animated" perspective. It was hard work, but it was fun and was certainly a perspective that creative and imaginative five and three-and-a-half year old siblings could relate to. And the positive results they saw in Genevieve were immediately reinforcing.

Before we knew it, and quite all of a sudden, Genevieve was talking! Maybe the timing was coincidental; but I don't believe it for a minute. For so long, we had watched as only the odd new word came from Genevieve's lips. Then out of the blue, she sang the ABC song. Kobe was so thrilled and proud that he smothered her with kisses! Genevieve went on to amaze us; when we watched "Mary Poppins" and to our absolute surprise, we realized that she knew and could sing almost all the words to "Chim Chiminy", in full sentences.

Genevieve had gone, literally, from near baby talk to speaking articulately, in complete phrases and often full sentences. It was beyond belief! Sydney, Kobe, Nolan and I marveled and pondered: Did she practice this stuff at night when no one was listening? We were absolutely astounded!

But as thrilling as it was, it was still heart-wrenching to acknowledge that Genevieve would happily say "Mary Poppins" and "Mickey Mouse", but very rarely "Mommy" or "Daddy". Why? When she had been a year old, she had frequently referred to us as "Mama" and "Dada"; yet now, at this time in her life, there was an odd refusal. There was clearly an innate discomfort deep within her that stopped her from enjoying us and reciprocating with us, on a social level. She would occasionally wrap her arms around us and give the sweetest kisses, but then poke our eyes and laugh. At the time, we tried to tell ourselves that it was her spunky personality and sense of humor; but it was of deep concern. Never would we have guessed it was indicative of the overwhelming level of social discomfort, distaste and overload she experienced because she had autism.

Genevieve could talk, she could sing; but she didn't understand social settings, even casual, everyday ones with her immediate family. Formal settings were even more confusing to her. One day, for instance, she watched as her uncle gave Sydney a hug good-bye; Genevieve dashed over, and struggled to remove his arms from her, because she thought he was trying to take away her sister. I could write pages and pages of examples of her social confusion and awkwardness.

As a family, we encouraged Genevieve to look at her reflection in our eyes, to increase her comfort level with being close and because we were desperate to make eye contact with her! It felt like she was looking not only at her own reflection, but beyond, right down to our toes. It didn't feel like she was looking at us, her family. We were more like objects of interest to her, something that she could study. She occasionally gave hugs, but they were brief, rather stiff and lacked warmth and genuine comfort level. If a friend or extended family member wanted to hug her, she would quickly turn around so that they could only hug her back and shoulders.

Yet, Genevieve stuck to me like glue and the amazing bond between us grew. Very early on, I could feel that I was the stepping stone from her world to ours.

Chapter 7

Despite the improvements in speech and the subtle signs of Genevieve's emerging peace with the world around her, by the age of three, she rebelled against structure of any kind. She constantly walked through our home, pulling toys and objects off the shelves, as if the mere appearance of structure and organization was repulsive and unnerving to her. She showed remarkable physical strength and determination and still, had no sense of danger.

The tantrums continued and if she was angry or frustrated, she would make a growling sound and bite her hand frantically, hard enough to leave teeth marks. In social settings, she would often spin in circles, making a horrid crowing sound, or just spin in silence. She had absolutely no ability to reason or to see another person's point of view. Her sleep patterns were bizarre and often she would stay up most of the night and continue on until bedtime the next night.

Her speech took on a new oddity: echolalia. We didn't know the term or even the concept at the time. Most of her speech lacked spontaneity and she echoed what she heard. For example, if she stumbled at the park, she'd say: "Are you okay?" Or if she was going down the slide and we asked: "Did you have fun, Genevieve?" she would answer: "Did you have fun, Genevieve?" At first we thought it was cute, and basked in the glory that at least she was talking and responding. We had no idea what that kind of speech issue was indicative of.

And yet, through it all, what continued to mystify and exasperate each of us, was the contrasts in Genevieve's behaviors. Despite the sheer intensity of the horrid moments with her, what stood out the most was her incredible sparkle and wonderful sense of humor. They shone through it all. She was, quite simply, captivating! Adults, children, everyone was mesmerized by her, by her spirit and by her perspective. As worried as we were about her, there was no denying that this girl was thriving. And as exasperated as we, and the world around her were by her bizarre and volatile behaviors, we were all equally mesmerized.

Picture if you will, Genevieve's presence at the baptism for her six month old brother, Hayden. The reverend did, as he always did at baptisms, ask for all of the children of the congregation to join him at the front while he performed the ceremony. There was Sydney; there was Kobe, along with a dozen other children, standing sweetly and orderly, like a flock of angels, next to tiny Hayden. Then there was Genevieve, with her long pink, princess dress and her tangled red curls (she rarely allowed us to brush her mass of long and unruly hair); she was spinning in circles. Nolan and I looked at each other, both holding our breath, thinking: "Oh, no!" We knew how she typically responded to overt social settings. We scrambled, wondering if we should run up and grab her and risk making a scene.

But there was no "crowing" or screaming coming from Genevieve's lips. And within seconds, another child started to spin, then another and another, until they all joined in! I remember ribbons. I'm not sure if Genevieve had brought them up with her or if Reverend Bob had given them out; but with all of these children spinning, ribbons in hand, they were like maypole dancers. It was beautiful, unexpected and completely random!

Luckily Reverend Bob was not thrown off, but simply put his hands up and like the rest of us, stood back and marveled at the sheer beauty and wonder of that amazing sight and those precious moments. It was like

Genevieve had an innate ability to touch each of us, to dare to let out a piece of our hearts and our souls. For some of the people present, it may have been a part they didn't even know they had. There was simply something in her that was just magic and effervescent!

Chapter 8

If you are reading this carefully, you may have suddenly asked yourself: "Baby brother Hayden...where did he come from?" Somehow, despite the chaos and all of the bizarre behaviors, I was able to convince Nolan that three kids were still not quite enough. Our fourth blessing arrived, shortly after Sydney turned five, Kobe three-and-a-half and Genevieve, two-and-a-half. I couldn't have been happier: four kids, barely five years apart. Now that would be a fun challenge and I was up for it. Nolan, very much a family man, was happy and also probably relieved to know that I had a high energy level and a lot of patience.

Sydney and Kobe were instantly in love with newborn Hayden, his red hair and his cleft chin. Genevieve amazed us by accepting him into her home and to our surprise, a new side of her poked through: a maternal side. But if I had met my match with Genevieve's behaviors, then Hayden would, in a short time, prove to be the ultimate challenge. More about that is to come. But to answer the question that may be running through your mind, as many people have asked me over the years: if I had to do it again, would I have gone for four? The answer is: absolutely. Would I have had them so close together, just five years apart? The answer is, again: absolutely.

But that is not to downplay the magnitude of what was going on. Hayden was born amidst a sea of chaos and the continual contrasts that had become our reality: incredible joy and sweetness, versus screaming and bizarre and stressful behaviors. That was our home, our existence, the mystery of who we were. What was wrong? Seriously, what was wrong?

We had four small kids; I couldn't imagine anyone having more love and sweetness in their lives than us. But we were loosing our minds. Unless you have endured hours of screaming, many times a day, everyday, for one and a half years, I'm not sure that you can really even begin to know what we endured and how emotionally scarred we were as a result. Sydney, Kobe and I were most affected. Even Nolan couldn't really grasp the severity because he wasn't there twenty four/seven, as we were.

Thankfully, Genevieve's effervescence often shone through so brightly, that it saved us from going completely over the edge. And Sydney and Kobe had incredible acceptance of our situation. I can hardly put into words how proud we were of them. They worked hard to gain Genevieve's trust. Her temper was becoming slightly more manageable, because we were learning to see the world through her eyes and to respond in ways that were safe to her. Also, we learned the "art of walking on eggshells". Through documenting and observing and looking from her perspective, we learned the things to avoid and how to respond, so as not to set her off. It truly was an art and we learned it well and we learned it quickly. What was not artistic was that though it brought results, it was stressful and draining, to always be on guard and to think before we spoke or responded to her, or we would pay a price.

Out of desperation, we continued to probe aspects of Genevieve's life, searching for explanations. One day, a thought popped into my head. I looked at my own body and my situation of dealing with extremely severe food and environmental allergies for a number of years. Then I looked at Genevieve. I listened to her scream; I acknowledged my state of exhaustion, not only because of her behaviors but because of her odd sleeping patterns.

It leapt out at me: could allergies be the problem? Maybe her constant red cheeks weren't just from teething. Kobe was very affected by allergies; maybe she was too. Filled with hope that I had solved the mystery and that an end might be in sight, we immediately put her on an elimination diet and were shocked at what we discovered. Literally, within twenty four hours of removing, in particular, wheat and dairy from Genevieve's diet, she was a different person. I remember bursting into tears of joy, saying: "My Genevieve is back!" That was when I realized exactly how much pressure and stress we'd been living with for such a long time. To have her back, calm, sweet and more affectionate, was an unbelievable dream come true. It was all I could think of.

We had her formally tested and were shocked to discover that her sensitivities were a virtual carbon copy of mine. At that point, I had been living, for two years prior, literally on rice and potatoes, with only the occasional addition of bananas, cauliflower and chicken. Fuelled by the improvements we were seeing in her, we kept her on a strict diet and spent months scrutinizing foods and her behaviors.

There were definite changes in her. Most noticeable was the significant decrease in tantrums and volatile behavior. She was happier and seemed more at peace with herself. She was more affectionate; her sleeping patterns became "normal" and I do believe there was a marked improvement in her speech. At home, we were consumed with keeping her on track, knowing we'd all pay a price if we "screwed up". We literally kept our fridge locked, using bungy chords; otherwise, at night Genevieve would sneak out of her crib and raid the fridge. If we found the ice cream scoop in her crib or smelled lasagna on her breath when she woke up, we'd be horrified by the realization that the next three days would be a nightmare!

Our efforts were well rewarded by the improvements we saw. The most fascinating change that we saw in Genevieve, that I do not believe for a second was just a coincidence, was specifically about her body. It was like her sense of "her body" was emerging! She was starting to *feel* sensations like pain and coldness. Until then, she had always been oddly oblivious to them. It was unforgettable, the first time she acknowledged an injury! I found her sitting in front of her mirror, scrutinizing a bruise on her arm. She was wrapped up in intrigue and fascination. It was like the little wheels in her head were turning, and she had suddenly discovered what it meant to have something on her skin and that it hurt. After that groundbreaking day, and for a long time to come, any time she sustained a bump or a bruise or a scrape, she would run to her mirror to check it out. And with respect to coldness and temperature: her awareness expanded to an acknowledgement about temperature. Sometimes, she would actually *ask* to wear a jacket!

Keeping Genevieve on a restricted diet was, however, terribly challenging. It was time-consuming and stressful. She had no way of understanding why she couldn't eat the things she loved, while watching other people around her eating and enjoying them. She became intensely frustrated. As a family, we omitted many foods, or at least, ate them only when she was not around because it broke her heart and ours to eat them in front of her. It was tough on Sydney and Kobe, as there were many foods they couldn't eat in her presence and many we couldn't even risk having in our home. For her siblings, there was a limit to the number of rewards and incentives we could offer *them* to "tough it out". At least seeing Genevieve calmer, happier, more talkative and responsive helped, but it was really tough.

We found it very frustrating, visiting friends and family, trying to make them understand that a bowl of cheesies or a plate of chocolate cake simply couldn't be left out where Genevieve could see it. As I had found with my own severe allergies, most people who are not affected, simply don't take them seriously and outright question the impact that can result. Even in Genevieve's case, most people did not understand the urgency of her strict diet. Many felt, and said, she should simply learn that she couldn't eat them, that they shouldn't have to be removed from everyone else. What were they thinking? For God's sake, she wasn't even three; what did they expect from her? And what did they expect from us, her family, who struggled to live with her?

Social functions became a huge issue and we drastically reduced our attendance; we carefully weighed out the pros and cons of taking her.

To many family members and friends, I finally gave graphic examples of her reactions to the severest foods, like chocolate. I described a toddler with a headache so severe that she would scream and cling desperately to me for hours; there would then be horrendous behavior to follow, usually for days afterwards. Tylenol helped, but we had to literally pin her down on the floor and force it into her. Finally, everyone started to get it.

Chapter 9

After eight long months of scrutinizing Genevieve's diet, Nolan and I were forced to admit that we had not completely solved "the mystery of Genevieve". There was no denying that we had made huge gains in many areas of her development and at least the massive headaches were not an issue when foods like chocolate were removed; and gradually, we had been able to successfully reintroduce small amounts of many foods back into her diet. But even when we kept her on a terribly restricted diet of rice, potatoes and ketchup, the truth was, much of the time she was miserable, screaming frequently and kicking us and objects for no apparent reason.

It was a complicated time and honestly, it was almost impossible to measure how much was allergies and how much was something else going on. She continued to exist so much in her own little world. She was a walking contradiction: when she wasn't screaming, she loved to laugh and say: "It's so funny!" It was adorable and it brightened our spirits; but those three words had the flavor of her "looking at" the world and finding it funny, as opposed to her "living in" the world and finding it funny.

Thankfully, the addition of baby Hayden now had a wonderfully, calming and peaceful affect on our home, a home that had endured far too much. Despite the stress of Genevieve's behaviors, she, Sydney and

Kobe were tightly knit in their unique way, like a litter of puppies. The five of us spent countless hours together, on the couch or in our big bed, feeding Hayden and snuggling. Genevieve could join us and flit in and out of her world as she pleased. It allowed her to address her need for isolation yet at the same time, bond with her new brother in her very unique way. She was surprisingly protective of him.

Feeding and snuggle time gave me lots of opportunity to spend quiet, meaningful and beautiful time with my little gang, each one of them lapping up the warm excitement and security that our home now exuded! But it was extremely challenging, meeting the constant demands of an infant, and three young siblings, all the while dealing with Genevieve's issues. If you were to take "snapshots" of us at that time, it was really quite bizarre. What you'd see would be hundreds of wonderful pictures of Genevieve riding Sydney like a horse, or the four of them, all piled into the bathtub, naked and laughing. You'd see Genevieve helping us paint a Christmas mural on the living room window; I could go on and on. But you'd also see as many, if not more, examples of her isolation, her aloofness and her volatile behaviors.

Yet somehow, as a family, it all worked. We had the magic glow that only a new baby in the house could give, and it saved us!

That amazing glow, however, soon became tainted. There was something very different about Hayden. I sensed it by his third week of life, though it was subtle and not an accurate warning of what was to come. I didn't make assumptions that he was following in Genevieve's footsteps, as his early beginnings felt completely different from hers; but something in the back of my mind told me to keep a close eye.

I started taking notes and it didn't take long to see curious and concerning patterns in Hayden's behaviors. Much of the time he was calm, happy and loving; but as much of the time, he fussed and was miserable, until I removed the two of us and we spent time alone. I knew it wasn't colic;

there was an intensity and urgency that didn't match colic. Right from the beginning, by his third week, I sensed that for some reason, it was "me and Hayden against the world", maybe not all of the time, but enough of the time. Within a few months, I was worried.

With Hayden, a new part of our journey had begun, though I couldn't have guessed at the time all that was to ensue. "A fork in the road" would be describing it too gently. The details are presented in his tale, *The Castle We Called Home;* but bits and pieces will make their way into this tale. The impact of Hayden and his presence in the life of our heroine would be fascinating but also, pervasive and profound.

Chapter 10

*G*enevieve was a force to be reckoned with, but she was truly emerging and there was much to be celebrated. Between the ages of three and four, echolalia was extreme. Looking back, her issues with speech were two-fold. She did not intuitively know how to put conversation together and to actually make it happen; plus she seemed to have an intrinsic desire to maintain a wall between herself and the people around her. Occasionally, she let down that wall. One evening, I was out and came home unexpectedly; when she saw me, she casually said: "Hi Mommy", like she had forgotten herself and her wall.

Another night, the only night that we had ever left the four of them anywhere for a sleepover, she was very upset at being left at her grandparents' house. She ran and hid behind the couch screaming very clearly and angrily: "I want my mommy!" You can hardly imagine how foreign it was for her siblings and grandparents to hear her speak that way. It was straight from her heart, with no echolalia and no walls. And she was actually acknowledging that she did need to have me in her life!

Genevieve continued to deal with social events and gatherings in one of three ways, or sometimes, a mixture of the three: she would either tune out and spin in circles, scream and/or "crow", or she would be like a fairy sprinkling pixie dust! At Thanksgiving Dinner, for instance, she held herself together by focusing on her own reflection on her wine glass. She innocently brought to our attention the fact that everyone's reflection was upside down and funny. Within moments, we were all studying our reflections, and they were like little wonders of the world that we would all have otherwise taken for granted. That was her: she pumped life and personality into everything. She did it to survive, and because she truly experienced the world differently.

With much coaching, cheering and praise, Genevieve learned to respond with: "Hi" and sometimes: "Please". She would beam with pride as she said each of our names. As a family, we cheered for her because we wanted her to feel proud of herself; but equally, we cheered because we were so genuinely thrilled. It felt so good to finally hear our names coming from her little voice.

Gradually, Genevieve was able to understand the concept of people, family members and the roles they played. Much of it was through movies and using animal figurines and sometimes dolls. In her private, solitary play, we noticed that she would assign them names, usually depicting the members of her family. It appeared that she was "trying them on for size" to see how it "felt" for her figurines, to interact with others. She was brilliant: she instinctively sought to learn and experience things *through* her toys!

Genevieve's relationship with us as a family was fascinating. She continued to see us more as an entity, than as individuals. She often struggled when it was not the six of us. Our emotions were such a mystery to her. One night for instance, I was annoyed with Sydney and Kobe's behavior (it was just typical kid stuff) and stormed out of the room. Genevieve immediately followed me and peered curiously into my eyes to see if I was crying. I could see the wheels in her mind turning, trying to figure it all out.

So much of the time, Genevieve appeared to care less if we were in her world or not; and yet she would go to pieces, screaming and crying, if one of us was upset, particularly if it was me. She was terribly inept at reading our emotions and yet at times, she was oddly insightful.

Her developing relationship with us as a family was heartwarming but certainly quizzical. We discovered that once we got the food issue under control, she seemed better able to bypass her distraught feelings and divert her energy into making it a personal challenge to cheer us up. She did it by making silly faces or giving hugs. This was a huge step, one filled with irony really, for someone with her history.

Hovering around us, Genevieve often appeared like she was trying to figure things out. One day she stumbled across Kobe, who was sick and had fallen asleep on the couch. She cautiously hovered around him and finally poked him, as if to see if he was still alive. To my surprise, she took it upon herself to find him a pillow and blanket, completely unassisted. That sort of behavior was, until then, simply unheard of. Studying her was fascinating, like a tightly woven and suppressed work of art that was slowly unraveling, revealing an even greater treasure within!

Fantasy continued to be our driving force in reaching Genevieve. More importantly, she was instinctively and very skillfully using it on her own. It was the beginning of a brilliant process and she moved mountains because of her personal skill and her phenomenal determination. On some levels, she was very much trapped in her world of fantasy, dressed in princess dresses and wrapped up in fairy tales and nursery rhymes. She was not simply acting the part, she was *being* the part. But there was no keeping this girl down and inch by inch, she was discovering that she could, quite literally, keep one foot in the safety of her world, while reaching out to ours, by using the safety of her fantasy world.

Though most of her playtime was still solitary, or at best, alongside her family as opposed to with her family, walls were lowering and breakthroughs were happening. Genevieve started to relate what she saw on TV and in Disney movies, to her relationships with Sydney and Kobe. She adored them and was, in her own way, very dependent on them. She would initiate play, through movie sequences and largely through dance. Picture Genevieve, in her "worn-practically-to-rags" Cinderella dress, waltzing with Kobe, to "Once Upon a Dream" from *Cinderella*. To her, it was a dream come true, to finally have her chance to dance with her brother, because he was handsome and very charming; but also because he was her real-life personification of the prince. She had watched many times before, when Sydney had taken the spotlight as his partner. Kobe was very proud of Genevieve's dancing accomplishment; but at the end of the song, when she puckered up looking for a dramatic and passionate kiss from him, her Prince Charming, he of course looked back in horror and declined. He was not, as she was, locked that deeply into Fantasy!

Genevieve's Cinderella dress was, quite literally, worn to rags. She wore it for weeks at a time and it wrenched her heart to the very depth of her soul if we tried to convince her to wear something else, even just long enough to wash it. What would have been the point in forcing the issue? At least she liked the person that she could present to the world, when she was dressed that way. And when she was contained within the dress and its blue and white thinning fibers, she could tiptoe out and face the world around her, much like an actor in a costume.

Over-stimulating activities with lots of people, noise and chaos were still a serious issue. Increasingly, Hayden was showing similar tendencies of responding either by tuning out, screaming or spinning in circles. A horrendous situation with one child was now being heightened by the addition of another. We were constantly faced by horribly stressful moments or incredibly wonderful ones, with rarely anything "average" in between. It was exhausting and completely overwhelming.

But some moments were so profoundly unique and beautiful, that it was impossible to be anything but fascinated. This is one of my favorites:

One hot summer day, Genevieve carted a huge jug of milk all the way over to the kitchen table. Hayden immediately pushed it over and the entire contents spilled over the table and onto the floor. Hayden, naturally, wanted to wade and splash in the pool of milk. Genevieve had little concern or interest. I was furious and frustrated and got on my hands and knees to mop it up. Obviously, I made Genevieve see and feel Cinderella. It was impossible to stay angry because when I looked in her eyes, I could see that at that moment, her mom was Cinderella! I practically felt like a celebrity, an animated character in the flesh!

How do I put what I saw in her eyes, on her face, and in her body, into words that will make sense to you? Genevieve experienced this incident on an entirely different level than her siblings would have. She was *watching* Cinderella in her own kitchen. I could feel it. Then I heard her sweet little voice singing: "Sing Sweet Nightingale", just as Cinderella had done in the movie as she mopped up her floor. *I was Cinderella*; and I could feel that Genevieve's acceptance of me in her life rose up a few notches because of that.

Genevieve experienced life very much on a sensory level. Her most intrinsically joyful activity was, as described at the beginning of her tale, lying on her tummy, dipping her hair in the mud puddles after a rain, as she spun around on a merry-go-round. She was in her sensory glory and was totally oblivious to the stares of the people around her. It was often exasperating to see how she could somehow find a mud puddle in any park and no matter what the size she could submerge herself in it!

Age four was a fascinating time of self exploration and world exploration for Genevieve. It was also a time of us exploring Genevieve! There was so much to learn from her and the unique perspective that she had. We felt it even back then, at that tender age; today, fourteen years later, we still feel it. Back then I saw it as such a loss for the people around her, who didn't take the time to learn from her, to step back and see the world through her eyes.

But like her family, most of the people in her world were captivated by her! I could write pages and pages. She was intelligent and despite her tendency to tune out the world, often appearing to be oblivious to things going on around her, she took it all in. Her peripheral vision and recall were staggering. In a single glance she could take in a level of detail that the rest of us would have missed or taken for granted. She processed and stored it all in her own unique way. She did watch everything and it was a constant intrigue to see how sometimes simple situations could baffle her and yet often, more complex ones, she was able to grasp fully.

One evening, for instance, all four kids were in the bath tub which was a favorite activity for each of them. Unthinking, and probably exhausted, I casually reminded Kobe that Hayden would need a hug the next day before he got his immunization shot. Sydney's feelings, naturally, were a little bit hurt as I had made her feel that Kobe was more special to Hayden than her. Meanwhile, Genevieve who was, as always, appearing to be dangling in her own little world, surprised us by lovingly wrapping her arms around Sydney's neck and hugging her. She had watched and taken in the whole thing and understood Sydney's hurt feelings. Sydney was ecstatic, feeling like she was the most loved person in the world.

Genevieve had an honesty that went beyond innocence; it indicated how differently she did process things. She would, for instance, constantly pull things off shelves and onto the floor and one day, the kids and I walked into a room to discover a huge mess. Annoyed, but knowing the answer, I asked: "Who did this?" Innocently and sweetly, Genevieve immediately piped up with: "I did it!" Sydney and Kobe's eyes were like saucers; they couldn't believe that she would own up to it. They laughed hysterically, knowing how hard they would have tried to cover up their crime, if it had been committed by them. The innocence was just so sweet but so curious because Genevieve didn't understand the concept of "lying". Sydney and Kobe still reflect on that incident today. They probably reveled on some level of glory when years later, Genevieve would learn that it was okay and socially "acceptable", to tell the odd little lie, though it certainly still does not come naturally to her.

By contrast to these moments and these experiences, much of the time, at four years of age, Genevieve was a hellion! She was still not toilet trained, and nothing we tried had any impact on improving that. At home, it was almost impossible to keep clothes on her, much less a diaper. Often, there she would be, sitting naked on the kitchen chair, with nothing but an open jar of peanut butter, a spoon and her adorable red, curly hair; or she'd be running through the house, wearing nothing but our Superman cape and crest. Even the lure of trying on my wedding dress, our ultimate "princess dress", wasn't more powerful than her desire to be naked. As Sydney and even Kobe covered themselves in my mass of white lace and tulle and pranced around the living room, Genevieve only paralleled them, in her naked glory.

When Genevieve would succumb to wearing clothes, most of her compromises were, of course, for costumes. And costumes we had! I did a lot of sewing back in those days. They were a part of our everyday life and our costume room was a magnet for neighborhood kids, who loved to join us in our world of make believe. Birthday parties and special occasions were a work of art and had become one of our family's trademarks. Armed with very little extra money but tons and tons of energy and imagination, we would dream up themes, with games, prizes, decorations and theatrics. To us, the possibilities were endless.

Through our parties, we were in our element, our glory and we worked as a team. In our home, it seemed like there was always paper mache drying or fabric being cut out. It was fun, exciting and a wonderful reprieve from the bizarre and stressful existence that otherwise filled our lives! At Sydney's *Alice in Wonderland* birthday, for instance, Genevieve was the Queen of Hearts; at the *Flintstones* party, she was Betty Rubble and at her own *Cinderella* party, she was, of course, Cinderella. Her cake was an actual pumpkin-shaped coach, with a photograph of Genevieve in the window. There were parties of Peter Pan, Pirates and treasures; the list went on and on.

Not all parties were a conscious effort to "reach" Genevieve; some of the motive was just because that was who we were. It was like breathing. But, as a tool for "bringing out" Genevieve, they worked powerfully and magically! She was so easily put off and overwhelmed by social activities and people, but she could somehow manage the wild, crazy and creative parties that were a part of her home environment. She would, at times venture out into our world and other times, stay in the safe glory of her own. What we were in essence teaching her, was to use her love and comfort level with fantasy, to tap into the security that she derived from it, and then enable her to navigate. We all saw it as a precious tool.

With open arms, Genevieve welcomed fantasy, and all that it encompassed, as a means of navigating into the world of others, but *equally* as a means of drawing people to her. It was a medium that was safe and non-threatening to her. It was a way that she could let them see the real her. As you will read in the chapters to come, she adapted it into her life brilliantly!

Outside of pre-arranged and carefully-orchestrated parties, interactions continued to be an enormous challenge and often our downfall. I still felt terrible guilt that I was neglecting Genevieve. I craved to spend time with her, to do "typical activities", like writing, drawing and painting. She would only allow it if I held the paint brush or the felt marker, with her hand overtop of mine. Through that activity, we discovered something new, although we were not familiar with the term or the concept at the time: perseveration. It would be another one of the determining factors in her later diagnosis of autism.

It was very curious that this child, who would flit disjointedly in and out of social contact, would engage with me in art activities, almost relentlessly. In our very first real "arts and crafts" experience together, Genevieve was glued to the activity for a solid two hours. She screamed incredibly afterward, not because she had been forced to maintain physical and social contact for so long, but because we had had to stop. She couldn't understand why we had to stop, and to her, it was like a spell had been abruptly broken.

Clearly that day, she could have gone on for hours and hours. Once again, how do I put this into words that will make sense and will describe the intensity and the uniqueness of the situation? Genevieve was so engrossed in the characters and the images we were creating, that she didn't want to leave them. They were that real to her and that much a part of her. And there was a fascinating sensory component attached to the activity as well. I sensed it was derived from the action of her holding my hand as we drew and cut out our paper creations; but also it was from the motion of our hands and from the pleasurable feel of my skin against hers'.

These drawing and creating experiences were ground breaking and took us in a new direction!

Chapter 11

Much about Genevieve was genuinely fascinating; but the fact remained that she was terribly hard to live with and we had so many concerns. Out of desperation, Nolan and I enrolled her in a local preschool. It wasn't just that we felt we needed help; it was that I needed time away from her. That in itself was painful to admit, as I'd never felt the need for a break from Sydney or Kobe.

Our preschool experience only heightened our frustration and anxiety, as well as our mistrust in bringing outsiders into our dilemma. Within the first fifteen minutes of Genevieve's attendance on her first day of preschool, she rebelled against their structured format and the presence of other children, by writhing and screaming on the floor. The preschool director curtly returned my stack of post-dated cheques and said it "wasn't going to work".

Genevieve and I left. I felt completely lost. To this day, I can't believe that the group of "professionals" in that preschool had no advice or support to give, not even a comment like: "Maybe you should get your local health unit involved or seek the advice of a pediatrician". Instead they gave nothing.

As traumatizing as the experience was, it did force a little recollection into my mind, about a friend's son who had been exhibiting some challenging behaviors. They had found a local preschool, with specially-trained staff and had seen great results. With fingers crossed, I called "Turning Point Preschool". Though the preschool was greatly in demand, typically with long waiting lists, they did have an opening for the following fall. That was, I have not a shadow of a doubt, one of our many little miracles! With fingers crossed yet more tightly, Genevieve and I went in for an observation. Within five minutes of observing the staff, their procedures and their immediate acceptance of Genevieve, I had absolute faith that finally, we were going to get some answers. It would be a long wait until the fall term; but I knew we were no longer in this alone.

That fall, the staff of Turning Point Preschool embraced Genevieve and all of her unique, curious and demanding behaviors with knowledge, sensitivity and caution. They didn't push her, particularly socially. They were content to let her parallel play with the other preschoolers, noting that she rarely acknowledged their presence, much less that of the staff.

Within the first few weeks of September, the Turning Point director sat me down and carefully tiptoed through her carefully-planned words, trying to gently present the staff's concerns that Genevieve should be classed as having special needs. From their level of experience, simply the fact that she was still not able to toilet train was an indicator. And there were, of course, many other indicators of concern.

My reaction was definitely not what the director had braced herself to receive. I was happy. I was relieved. I asked her to stop tiptoeing around and to just tell me what their impressions were. Finally, we could get moving on this! From where I stood, I had a sister who was schizophrenic; I had a brother who had become a paraplegic when he was eighteen. I had a sister who had died of polio at the age of four and a large family who had struggled to recover from the loss. I had a brother affected by Down syndrome, whom I loved and had helped to raise as though he were my own son. I had learned that people could be different, and could deal with challenges and still lead unique and meaningful lives. I wasn't afraid of the staff's assessment of my daughter. I wasn't going to waste time and energy in denial and anger. I just wanted to know what the problem was and get moving!

The bottom line was, for me, that I already knew something was different and that there were challenges ahead; I had been documenting behaviors for many, many months. I saw a daughter who was enormously challenged, but I also saw a daughter who was captivating, gifted and incredibly determined. I saw her sparkle and her potential. That was all I needed. I knew her life would be different from what it would have otherwise been, but I didn't doubt for a moment that she would have a good life.

We'd already started the journey. From my perspective, it had started that day in my sister Charlize's home. Now, at last, people would have to listen.

Chapter 12

By the beginning of October, the child psychologist connected to Turning Point Preschool gave us his assessment and subsequent diagnosis: autism. Though I was prepared for an assessment indicating a significant level of severity in Genevieve's development, it was like walking into a wall. Even his kind eyes, his gentle nature and his warm and fatherly beard did little to buffer the blow. It was one of those surreal experiences where it hit so boldly that I remember exactly what I was wearing that day.

I think more than anything, I was dumbfounded because I had studied autism briefly in university and what I saw there wasn't what we saw in Genevieve. Obviously, ten years prior, autism was only acknowledged in the most severe terms.

It *was* like walking into a wall, but I was oddly relieved that Genevieve had a diagnosis that was "significant enough" that she would get help; she wouldn't be one of those kids who "fell through the cracks". Doors would open for her because of her diagnosis. It was a shock, but finally we had the answer, the missing piece to the puzzle that had intrigued and exasperated us for so long. My very next thought was (and you would be shocked to hear how many people, even people I barely knew, have asked me this over the years): "If we do this right, this will hold the six of us together in a way that would not otherwise be possible. I *can* do this and I *will* do this".

From where I stood, it was indeed time to roll up our sleeves and get moving. But I was not anticipating the stumbling block of having to defend the diagnosis to family, friends and even my own husband. Apparently they all knew more than the trained professionals involved. Knowing enough to look deeper, I could see the reality that was written behind their lines and see that they were in shock and in denial. They didn't have the benefit of growing up as I had done, in learning to accept and embrace. It was annoying and something I had little time and desire to address; and it regretfully added to the load of all that was to be done. But it was, to some degree, (and as I have since found in working with other families), quite predictable. It just wasn't something that I subscribed to and it eventually became part of the motivation behind writing this book.

From the day Genevieve was diagnosed, I felt adamant that as a family, we should never be afraid to use the word autism, that it should be a part of our everyday vocabulary. We couldn't push her through life "hoping no one would find out". The image was so clear to me: we had to grab this bull by the horns so to speak, and educate Genevieve, ourselves and the world around her, about autism and about whom she was and how it affected her.

It was crystal clear to me that this was a pervasive disorder; but it wasn't all negative. She was amazing and that was what I wanted to focus on. Let the world see her in all her sweetness and spunk, so that they could say to themselves: "Wow, I had no idea a person with autism could be so loving and so captivating!" It would be a fine line between "branding her" with a label and that of educating and enticing the world to see her for whom she was: both amazing and pervasively challenged. Two and a half years of documenting and analyzing her behaviors had proven to me that she truly was an astounding person, and much of that was because she had autism. No matter how well she might do in life, autism was a part of whom she was and how she interpreted life and consequently, how she responded to it.

Already I found myself walking a fine line. Even replaying the words of the child psychologist, the day he gave his diagnosis made me feel nagging contradictions between his words and what I felt in my experiences with Genevieve. He had emphasized that though there was no known cure for autism, dealing with it was an issue of "altering and modifying behaviors through strict behavior management". Parts of his advice did not sit well with me. Yes, of course there were behaviors that made Genevieve's life and ours terribly difficult and needed to be delicately addressed; but what right did we have to dismantle what was such an intimate part of her?

I felt certain that half the trick would be for Genevieve to feel safe and accepted and that that would be the most powerful tool in enabling her to thrive and take off.

And what would be the best way to make her feel safe? In my mind, it was to accept her for who she was, and to let the people around her see and feel her sparkle and her uniqueness; that would entice them to want to be a part of her life and her journey. As a family, we would walk a very fine line between being sensitive to her self image and her right to privacy, and that of being open about her diagnosis. But I felt absolute clarity and conviction in the need for it. I was driven by it. It simply made no sense to me, as I watched her float and navigate through life, to subscribe to the prevalent philosophy which seemed based on the belief in stomping out behaviors and modifying behaviors well enough to make the child *appear* to be able to squeeze in and "fit" in amongst their peers.

In those weeks following Genevieve's diagnosis, as I formatted in my mind the route that was spilling out of me, I knew it contradicted popular beliefs and that represented another element that would haunt and loom over me. But I lived the way I did; I grew up the way I did; and the one thing I had learned, was to listen to my heart and to trust my instincts. At the end of the day, this was our child and our family. By the time Genevieve was grown up, the people involved with her now would have moved on to different families or different avenues.

We would still be here and we would have to feel, whether we had been successful or not, that at least we had done what we had felt were right for her and right for us, as a family.

As parents, having a formal diagnosis also brought three things to light that we knew we had to address immediately. The first, was presenting to friends and family why we would now need to be very particular about the commitments we could make to social events, and to the time and emotional support we could offer to anything outside of our immediate family. Also, we needed to evaluate our financial situation because it was clear that we would be living under one salary for a very long time. That was a concern because we should have been at a place, as many of our friends were, where I could have been able to supplement our income with part-time work of my own.

The third and most vital to each of us, was to make it very clear that we were not looking for sympathy from anyone, because we did not, or have we ever since those early days, considered our situation to be one that warranted sympathy. All we asked for was understanding and support.

During that "exploratory time", those few months after Genevieve was diagnosed, two tiny but magical little experiences gave me images, important images that I trained myself to recapture and draw upon when I needed to have a shot of patience and understanding with Genevieve. They revived me with compassion and respect for her and all that she had to deal with, to turn my anxiety and frustration into fascination and insight.

In their simple ways, these two little experiences were life altering. The first happened on a day when the kids and I stood waiting in line at a department store cashier. I happened to look up and noticed a convex security mirror strategically placed near the ceiling. At seeing our distorted images, I noticed how oddly strange and mildly disorientated it made me feel. It hit me: maybe that was something like what it felt for someone with autism, especially when he or she was in a building like this, with its multitude of sights, sounds, scents and above all, people. I pointed it out to Sydney and Kobe and I could see that it caused them to step back and ponder as I had done. It gave each of us a lasting image that was deeply meaningful.

The second magical moment hit a couple of months later, when Nolan and I were watching the movie *Wolf* in which Jack Nicholson played a man with wolf-like abilities. Amongst other senses, he had a heightened sense of sight, sound and taste which were completely overwhelming to him when he was surrounded by people and urban settings. The impact caused him to feel threatened, territorial and aggressive. It instantly made me think and feel Genevieve. She had a long history of being supersensitive to sensory stimuli one minute, yet other times, seemingly oblivious and unaffected. The images from this movie helped me take a bigger step into her head and her body, and filled me with yet more respect and awe.

Both experiences and images were incredibly powerful; they were tools. And we became masters at using tools!

Chapter 13

The Turning Point Preschool staff changed our lives, not only with their insight and patience, but their unwavering support to Genevieve, to me and to our entire family. Slowly and uniquely Genevieve excelled. She was assigned a key worker named Shyla who took Genevieve's lashing out, biting and pinching in her stride for months. Gradually Genevieve's acceptance of the staff and her new environment grew.

When the Turning Point staff embarked on toilet training, using a slightly different perspective than all of the methods we had tried, Genevieve was trained in three days. Socially her behavior remained very aloof; yet to watch her, you would never have guessed, how closely she watched everyone and everything that was going on around her. In tiny steps, she began to join in with the circle sing-along and she knew all the words. It was an amazing sight, to see her singing, despite the fact that she still kept a wall up between herself and the other children. But the staff remained respectful of that wall and didn't push her.

After many months we had a breakthrough, a big one! It was the first time Genevieve acknowledged the presence of another child. She and I had just stepped into the preschool; she walked over to a little boy and said: "Hi boy!" Then she did the same to another and then a third. I slipped outside and cried.

Consistency between home and school was crucial and we could see very early on, that teamwork and constant feedback between us and the staff was very powerful. Overall, Genevieve came to enjoy preschool but she deeply resented the fact that it reduced her time at home with me. And often I paid a price when she came home, as she would be mentally and physically exhausted and overwhelmed.

The age of four was truly a monumental, pivotal time in Genevieve's life. But it wasn't just the work we had done as a family prior to her diagnosis. It wasn't just the staff and the accepting environment at preschool. It wasn't just that we all altered our expectations and perspectives to allow her to emerge. *It was Genevieve.* She was working hard. She was climbing mountains that most of us reading this book can barely even imagine. At this moment as I look at what I've written, and I look at who she is now at the age of eighteen, I'm fighting back tears because this girl has worked so damn hard! She is a true inspiration. Her determination and sincerity are like nothing I've ever seen before.

I think back to those early years when we would encourage Genevieve to gaze into our eyes, especially me, because I was so desperate to feel that connection with her. Even though I knew she was looking through me, I knew that she was astute enough to take in parts of me and my soul, even if only subconsciously. What a connection she and have shared and how it has grown over the years. I am so deeply blessed.

Genevieve wanted desperately to communicate and she deserved most of the credit for the steps she took to accomplish that goal. I'm not sure that I can put this properly into words, to do her justice; but I do believe that even at the very young age of four, she had insight well beyond her years. She *knew* that if "Mommy was her stepping stone" then Fantasy, movies, fairy tales and nursery rhymes were the bridge. They held the key, and her strategy and process were brilliant. I am desperate to make anyone reading this book, understand that this was not simply a child wrapped up in the rapture of literature, movies and images. She skillfully, and with a semi-formatted plan, and a course of action somewhere in her mind, incorporated them into her life and her own personal journey!

Disney movies were the most immeasurably valuable tools for her. Genevieve watched them repetitively, usually all on her own. She was not perseverating; she was watching, learning and growing. *She was working and she was only four years old!*

I do believe that Genevieve *was* working, that she had a plan and that much of the reason that she was now lashing out at the world less frequently and with less intensity, was because she felt loved and accepted. She knew that her uniqueness was embraced. She was then able to channel much of that explosive energy more positively, into self exploration and "human-nature" exploration. *I believe to the depth of my soul, that the greatest gift and the single most significant form of therapy she has ever received, has been acceptance, of letting her see and feel that our goal was not to force a "square peg into a round hole".*

It was fascinating to observe Genevieve watching movies. Through repetition, she taught herself to connect certain words and phrases with the actions and expressions made by the characters; she then incorporated them into her own life. By kindergarten, she would have a vast repertoire of "chunks" of phrases to use. Sometimes they were bang on; sometimes they didn't fit accurately, which proved our suspicion that she often didn't understand what she was saying, but that the chunk roughly fit the circumstances, so it worked.

Years later, I would discover a quote from an autistic woman who said: "You learn how to manipulate language to make people think that you know what you're talking about". By five years old, Genevieve would be doing it brilliantly, and with the same inflection as the character onscreen. For example, we knew if her dialogue was a "chunk" from Belle in *Beauty and the Beast* as opposed to Judy Jetson in *The Jetsons*. For a girl who barely spoke until she was three, she had developed an uncanny ability to watch the characters onscreen, to listen, to take in their dialogue, observe how they reacted and how other characters then responded to them, and then relate it to her own true-life experiences. It was simply phenomenal.

What Genevieve saw onscreen was received by her as intimate, personal and very real. For example, she once pressed her face against the TV screen, to enable herself in her own mind and her own body, to actually "stand under the umbrella" with Christopher Robin. Another time, she spent twenty minutes watching *Beauty and the Beast* from the reflection in her dad's glasses. There was just something so extraordinary in her perspective; it would never have occurred to Sydney and Kobe to experience a movie in either of those ways. In the *Beauty and the Beast* scenario, she seemed to enjoy the physical closeness with her dad, but felt curiously "shielded" from his presence because she had his glasses to keep him separate from herself. In some respects, he was like an instrument that enabled her to experience something that was precious to her, namely the movie and its beloved characters who were her friends; but she could experience it from a new dimension.

Genevieve very much "lived" the characters that she saw onscreen and used them as navigational tools. With their help and their "presence" via their dialogue and their personalities, she felt safer around people. Gradually in tiny steps, she acclimatized herself to be around others a little bit more. Characters and the countless scenarios that she studied, not only enabled her to experience how to use language to communicate, they helped to teach her how to understand people, their emotions and their actions, all of which were confusing to her. Some plot scenarios inspired her to recreate the same within her own life, making them a mixture of playful, real-life re-enactments and a further study in her quest for understanding human nature.

One dinnertime for instance, we were eating spaghetti and Genevieve was very deep in character. She shared a single strand of spaghetti with her dad, exactly as Lady and the Tramp had done in their movie, their faces drawing closer and closer as each nibbled away at their end of the strand. It was a magical and very indicative picture of who Genevieve was at the time, which we luckily captured on film. There was a glow in her eyes and a look of sheer delight that told us how real and how important that moment was to her. She *was* Lady, and she felt everything that she knew Lady had felt in *her* "Italian restaurant" moment. She also seemed to revel in the fact that she could be physically close to her dad, while maintaining that all-important inanimate object (the strand of spaghetti), between them to buffer the "socialness". After, in the blink of an eye, she left the dinner table. We suspected she probably had another magical movie moment that she craved to relish in her own private world. And likely, she also needed to offset the close proximity she had shared with her dad, with private, solitary time, to "brush off the remains" that might be left on her clothes or her skin from that intimate experience with him.

Similarly, when Genevieve had watched *Beauty and the Beast* through the reflection in Nolan's glasses, I don't think she was motivated simply by the odd perspective the reflection gave her; it was deeper than that. She seemed fascinated by the feeling that she could be physically close to someone, but that the glasses provided a wall that kept her safely separated from them. In many ways, we, her family, were like pawns or objects that she could use to make her fabulous fantasies and explorations real. She could use us to pursue her own zest for understanding people, who were the curious creatures that surrounded her. We could see it and we could feel it. It was quite bizarre, like nothing we had ever seen or experienced; but it was breath-taking and fascinating! It meant the world to us that we were chosen to be a part of it.

Some of the "chunks" from movies were raw and very much indicative of the insecurity and angst that Genevieve felt when she was not in the safe haven of her home. The most memorable for Sydney, Kobe and me, was the time we were in a large and very busy drug store. I was focused on attending to Hayden and asked Sydney and Kobe to retrieve Genevieve, who had walked a little bit ahead of us. As they both tried to gently take her hand, she lashed out at them, screaming loudly, something like: "Let me out of here!" She used a snarling voice that was decidedly that of the outraged and cornered Beast, from *Beauty and the Beast*. It drew gasps and stares from the many people around us! The fact that the two children trying to coax her were young and were obviously siblings thankfully alleviated their fears that she was being abducted. It was an experience I doubt that any of us will forget; and it was one of many.

Some of the movie scenarios re-enacted by Genevieve were for her personal pleasure and fulfillment, as well as social escape. One of my favorites happened on a lovely, summer evening when we were visiting our next-door neighbors, out in their yard. Socially, Genevieve couldn't join in playing with her siblings and their friends, so she would typically tune them out and instead, "crawl into a movie scene". That evening, she literally crawled under a hedge, like a cat. She *was* a cat, a Siamese, again from *Lady and the Tramp*. She sang, straight from her heart: "We Are Siamese", radiant in her feline glory. Though her knees and tummy were scratched and bleeding, she didn't care; she was a Siamese cat entrenched in her adventure! The prickly hedge and the rocks and dirt below made it all the more real, and also shielded her from the overwhelming "social strings" of the evening.

It was always amazing to observe not only how Genevieve re-enacted these scenes, but *why* she felt the need. She was listening to her heart and to her body and she was forging out a path. It's what I saw in her, and what I was consequently so inspired to take her lead with. I saw it then and it has certainly been confirmed now in her teenage years, by comments and recollections she has made of those earlier years and her fascinating explorations.

Amongst Genevieve's unique talents was an extraordinary ability to memorize movies, word for word, from start to finish. Her skill astounded us and exasperated us! Sydney, who shared bunk beds with her, bore the greatest brunt. Frequently at 4:00am, Sydney would wake us up to say: "Mommy, Genevieve's reciting the entire *The Land Before Time*...again!" (for the second time that night). Though Sydney was exhausted and frustrated, we could see that she was also utterly fascinated.

Movie characters truly were as real and as meaningful to Genevieve as any real-life person, plus they had the bonus that they did not have the same "social strings attached". If I were to choose the single, most memorable and amazing moments in those early years, it would be the *Nutcracker Prince* episodes. A number of times I crept down to the living room at 3:00am to find Genevieve, dancing magically, swishing in circles with her little arms wrapped lovingly around our nutcracker. She was living a scene from the movie, and she recited the dialogue, word for word, inflection and all.

Those adventures were not simply a child's sheer delight in acting out a tempting movie scene. They were proof of a complex, gifted child's need and desire to explore the "world of people, of language and of feelings". It was a world that Genevieve knew she was barely a part of, but desperately wanted to be. I was blown away by her intellect, her perceptiveness and determination, and equally, by the way she perceived life. I believed with all my heart, and still do, that she instinctively knew that she needed to teach herself how to speak, to socialize, to fit in and to make sense of it all.

She chose methods that were a part of who she was, that were meaningful, safe and irresistible. How do I express how much it meant to me to be the person she chose to reach out to, to sometimes bring into her world? As for the *Nutcracker Prince* episodes: I don't think words have been created yet, to describe what it was like to witness those precious moments when she danced with our nutcracker, her heart and her soul glowing! Each time, I was torn between the temptation and desire to let her know that I was there, so I could become a part of her fantasy, contrasted by the concern that I had no right to impose. It was her fantasy, her exploration and a place that she needed and deserved to have all to herself!

Years later, when at the age of sixteen, I asked her about those 3:00am explorations, she remembered them vividly and fondly!

Genevieve's unique take on the world was complemented by her insatiable appetite for learning and an intrinsic desire to create. Already at the age of four, we pictured her as a fantasy writer when she grew up. She could perform puppet shows and converse with us through them. Sometimes she could even switch roles and become the audience while she watched us perform. This important work carried on into day-to-day situations, at times making her willing and able to answer: "Yes" or "No" to our questions. As a family, we could occasionally have little bits of conversation with her, though we had to work very hard and skillfully, and they were not particularly spontaneous on her part.

Occasionally, Genevieve would now answer me with: "Thank you, Mommy", though it was only in a whisper. It was indescribably delightful to hear those words pass through her little lips! I suspected that the fact that they were always in a whisper was her way of "meeting me halfway".

Sydney and Kobe were thrilled at the responses they were getting from Genevieve and they continued to be very quick studies. Instinctively they took it upon themselves to drill her on new concepts and skills. For example, one week we were focusing on the concept of "or" and both kids were tireless and endlessly creative in their efforts. They constantly drilled her with questions like: "Genevieve, is this big or small?" or "Genevieve, is it fun or sad to be sick?" The results were amazing, as was their growing relationship with her.

Though Genevieve's speech was still predominately echolalic, there were times when "she got it". One night at bedtime, I casually said: "Goodnight my little girl", anticipating her echolalia response of: "Good night my little girl". To my disbelief and complete surprise, she responded with: "Good night my little mommy". She had gotten it! The significance of that moment should not be lost or taken for granted. Those few words marked an important turning point in this autistic child's ability to understand language, to use language and above all, to feel *safe* enough to let it all come together. On a camping trip, she amazed us when she whispered sweetly to her grandparents who had joined us: "Thank you for coming". Wow!

Fascinating little milestones and discoveries abounded everywhere. Tiny, everyday things that we as parents, and Sydney and Kobe as "typical" kids took for granted, were in Genevieve terms, distinct and brand new. One beautiful example was the actual night that she discovered for the first time, the moon and the stars from her window. Until then, they had really never registered on her. For some reason, that night they entered her life; she was mesmerized and sweetly sang: "When You Wish Upon a Star". It then took her the longest time to settle herself down to sleep!

Chapter 14

Contrary to Genevieve's intense desire to "be" the characters that she saw onscreen and heard about in nursery rhymes, she was at last, gradually willing to wear clothes, beyond the two or three princess dresses that had dictated her wardrobe for so long. That in itself was proof that honoring her connection with her fantasy world made her feel more accepted and less anxious. She no longer *needed* to be dressed in character to the intense level that she did before. She didn't have the same incessant and desperate need to protect herself from the world around her. When she showed signs of being able to tolerate overalls or a few other outfits, we didn't push it. Instead, we'd buy three identical outfits and then a fourth that was very slightly different. Gradually, she accepted the variances and branched out. It was an important measure of her growing sense of security and trust in us.

Genevieve was the embodiment of more sweetness and curious behaviors, than I can put into words, except to say that she truly was an effervescent angel, whose feet never quite touched the ground. Bit by bit, she brought herself into our world. Frequently in the morning, she would climb down to Sydney's bunk and whisper: "Syd, wake up!" Sydney, though desirous of more sleep, was thrilled. What a breakthrough. And the bond between Genevieve and Kobe, both so close in age, also blossomed. Sometimes I'd see them snuggled up on a pillow together, their "magic carpet", as they watched *Aladdin*.

Wonderful, vibrant moments: there were countless numbers of them. And yet, we lived every moment, knowing that in the blink of an eye Genevieve could erupt like a volcano!

As her family we learned, if only out of desperation, how to respond to keep her calm. But also, we were driven because it made her so genuinely happy to have serenity in her life. We learned, as did she, an immensely powerful navigational tool: the art of collecting. It began with Dr. Seuss books. If we took her shopping in a mall, we were all pretty much guaranteed a delightful adventure if she was allowed to seek out and buy one Dr. Seuss book. It took awhile for us to see the pattern and to understand what was going on; but what she was doing, from a very young age, was acknowledging that her body could not tolerate the sensory and social bombardment of a mall, unless she had something tangible and meaningful to focus on. She literally had to be able to hold onto that item, to feel it in her hands, within her body and her soul; then she could manage awesomely. Otherwise, she would be pushed over the edge and the result would be a full-blown autism meltdown. Many people within the autism community believed (and many still do), that allowing an autistic child to indulge in his or her fixations would cause irreparable damage. That was not our experience, not when fixations were treated delicately and as a tool. With insight and scrutiny, they could be guided into something constructive and very powerful. By focusing energy and attention on the object of fixation, Genevieve, like other children with autism, could block out the stimuli that would otherwise overwhelm her over-active nervous system.

From our vantage point, the art of collecting was indeed a tool. At times, it may have gotten out of hand and certainly we quickly became aware of another autism trait, that being "obsession"; but you have to remember that at this point, we were dealing with the very complex behaviors of not just one, but two autistic children. I don't feel that Genevieve *ever* abused or took advantage of our willingness to accept collecting as a strategy. She used it because she needed to and stopped using it when she was old enough and safe enough to venture out without it. I can prove that by jumping ahead to the present for just a moment: recently, when Genevieve and I were interviewing Juniper, a new life skills worker, somehow in our conversation Juniper mentioned Dr. Seuss. By the end of the interview, Genevieve was visibly shaken and unnerved. She later revealed to me, with a quivering voice and tears in her eyes, that though she liked Juniper and was looking forward to spending time with her, the conversation and the reference to Dr. Seuss in that context triggered very painful memories of difficult times. She remembered that Dr. Seuss books were the first thing that she started collecting and "obsessing" about. The conversation had not only reminded her why she had needed to collect them, but also how far she'd come. With yet more tears, she articulated that the conversation stirred up within her, feelings of how incredibly hard she had had to work for so many years and how difficult the road had been.

How much more proof does anyone need, to see that this brilliant girl was the driving force behind her own success and emergence, into a world that was pervasively challenging to her? I call her story and her life's journey a tale; if that is true, it is a monumental tale and Genevieve is a true heroine!

During the elementary school years, Genevieve often talked *through* her collections and fixations, as a means of communication. At school whether they were a series of books, a line of animal figurines, a favorite singing group or characters on a TV show, fixations truly were a double-edged sword. She constantly teetered between her fixations drawing people to her, and fixations pushing them away, because her social anxiety and discomfort caused her to delve into them too deeply. Even when she had school friends over and was in the safety of her home, her muddled emotions, joined with her difficulty in conversing, often translated into her making repetitive remarks like: "It was funny in the Simpson's when…" At first, her friends seemed to think it was cute but after a short while, when it continued, they looked back at her with bewilderment and frustration.

There were many points in Genevieve's earlier life when we, her family, were driven to the point of absolute exasperation when she would go on and on about her fixations and expect us to keep up. In recent years, she has become conscious enough to keep her comments limited. Back then fixations did fill a void in her conversations which is sometimes noticeable now, as she has became more aware of the negative affects they may have. At eighteen, she is more inclined to leave the conversation, often vacating the room, rather than letting herself get caught up in fixation rhetoric.

Back then, Archie comics had also become a passion, a new navigational tool and means of exploring the curious world of people and their personalities. Genevieve often spoke as if she herself was a comic character, putting her thoughts and observations together as if they were from the bubbles and captions. In everyday conversation for example, she would say things like: "and then Sydney revealed to me that she and Dad had admitted…"

I saw Genevieve's fascination with comics as another little door that opened up, to reveal to us, a new aspect of the very fascinating ways in which her mind and body worked. It opened our eyes yet more to how she experienced life and how she responded to it. I don't think it was a "little" door at all; it spoke volumes and it seemed as plain as day to me that beyond the artwork and the drawings that held such an appeal, there was something about cartoons that was to her, insightful but "controllable". She told me that she wished she could be a cartoon. I suspected it was because cartoon life was very pure and simple. The characters' lives were flat, with minimal interactions with other characters, and their lines and their lives were scripted. There wasn't the onslaught of chaos and human emotion that was a part of real life. And cartoon characters were safe; they never died or had more than short, interactive dealings with life or its challenges.

When Genevieve was about eleven, she made a comment that was cute but curiously deep and insightful, especially coming from someone who had had to work so hard and had dealt with many serious obstacles. She said simply: "Life is a comic. Make it funny!"

Chapter 15

As fate would have it, this tale was not just about Genevieve and certainly not at this point in her life. If every heroine must have an antagonist, she found hers' in Hayden. We all did. His behaviors were horrendous! He had a serious impact on all of our children, but most seriously on Genevieve. She was, afterall, an autistic child with her own pervasive challenges, struggling to live with a complex and very aggressive, autistic brother. And Hayden was relentless towards her, because her passive nature made her an easy target and because he was fascinated by her. He wanted to play with her. To complicate the picture, he was terribly territorial towards me and was deeply threatened by the intense bond that Genevieve and I shared.

Life in our home was a daunting challenge. Some days I was filled with energy and optimism; other days, I felt that my heart was truly broken. Each day meant intense levels of chaos and unanswered questions as to Hayden's behaviors and what to do about them. I felt that I had such deep insight and direction into whom Genevieve was but that didn't change the reality that her situation alone was complex and pervasive. And now as a family, we had two of them, pushing us to unbearable limits. Yet as always, the rough and the horrendous were alternated with captivating charm, warmth and sweetness. Perplexing is only one of the dozens of words that would fit into the description of our home and our lives.

Though Nolan and I were still so much in love with each of our four children, it was an impossible way to live. Genevieve and Hayden had shared wonderful moments together when he was very young; but by the time he was two and a half, and she was five, she had seriously detached herself from him. We literally could not even say "Genevieve and Hayden" in the same sentence, even if it was whispered, without her going berserk. The mere sight of their backpacks set down and touching each other was enough to put her over the edge. Having autism meant that she experienced life on a very literal and physical level and his aggressive, and often relentless behavior stopped her from acknowledging the moments when he was adorable, sweet and loving.

Yet somehow, she continued to evolve.

Within Genevieve, a new talent emerged: she began to draw. She took to it like wildfire, and it was hard to believe that until the age of four, putting a pencil or felt pen in her hand seemed excruciating to her, like we were forcing her to grasp a repulsive object. Little wonders continued to abound. Just as she turned five, we happened to pick up a huge chalkboard at a neighbor's garage sale. We brought it home and watched with our jaws open in complete shock and surprise, as she walked over to it, picked up a piece of chalk and printed out the entire alphabet! Nolan and I then saw in her, a fascination with letters which was all the more amazing considering the fact that prior to that moment, she had refused all of our attempts to try printing. Six months prior to that day, she would have screamed and shook if I had even tried to get her to hold a pen, much less ask her to attempt to print the alphabet. Writing on the chalkboard that day, her letters were rough and shaky, but they were legible and each was purely from memory. This was another ground-breaking moment! I just stood and cried.

Genevieve's creative play was also changing. Instead of thrashing Barbie dolls and biting and mutilating their hands and feet, she now played appropriately with them. It was interesting that she never bit or damaged any of her dozens and dozens of animal creatures and figurines. I suspected that until then, Barbie dolls were still too "human" and too socially intrusive to be comfortably brought into her world of play; but as her comfort level with the world around her increased, we saw it reflected in her play.

Chapter 16

The age of five also brought about another new world to be explored and conquered, one with countless "social strings attached": elementary school. As parents, it meant more soul searching and more items on the growing list of stressful and difficult decisions that were becoming common place to us, but nothing that any of our "typical" friends could relate to. We knew that the wrong decision could have life-long effects.

"Should we choose the very large school that was further away but recommended for Genevieve's specific needs, or the small school close to home, with the heart-warming history of two resource rooms, and several mainstreamed special needs children?" After months of weighing out and agonizing, our final decision was made the moment we walked into the smaller school, called Amity Elementary.

There truly was something magical within the walls of Amity; we could feel it instantly. It started from the principal and worked its way down through the staff and right down to the students themselves. It was a school that felt like a family and it was a place where the special needs component was embraced. Acceptance and awareness were cultivated every day in subtle and well-planned ways, right down to opportunities for typical kids to experience what it was like to be in a wheelchair or needing to be spoon fed.

In a heartbeat, we jumped at the chance to be a part of this environment. It felt so right, even if it meant pulling Sydney and Kobe out of their existing school and starting anew. It wasn't an easy request, asking them to leave their many school friends behind; but like us, they were able to look at the big picture and, I think, they saw it as a way of embracing the journey that lay ahead. But I do remember, the sadness in Kobe's eyes as I left him on his first day of grade one, at our new school. He looked so lost; but by the end of the morning when I came to pick him up, he came bursting out of the school, proudly exclaiming: "I did it; I made a new friend!" And on he, and Sydney went from there.

With Genevieve now in tow, it was an incredible sight, watching the three of them holding hands and frolicking each day, to their new school. Both Sydney and Kobe had exceptional teachers, and for Genevieve, our unique lover of Fantasy, there awaited a kindergarten teacher and a special education assistant who both radiated with energy, insight and imagination. They could feel Genevieve's sparkle and she responded cautiously, but whole heartedly to them and the program that they offered.

There were ups; there were certainly downs, but we worked constantly as a team. We guided and modified where we felt necessary. Overall, Genevieve's classmates were even more captivated and drawn to her than she was to them! She was like a wildflower, blooming and radiating. But she was very much on her own unique and curious wavelength. Often, she struggled to survive amongst the more "cultivated flowers" around her. She desperately wanted to fit in but her individuality was precious to her and so she scrambled to preserve her unique spirit and independence.

Morning transitions from school to home were sometimes tough and often Genevieve went to school a mess of long, tangled, red hair lassoed into a ponytail. Sometimes she'd go an entire week without brushing it. She looked like she was neglected, but from where we stood, we learned from experience not to push the small issues. Once when I had pushed the issue and tried to brush her hair before school, she missed the following three days because it had pushed her over the edge. On the rare days when her hair was brushed, it was wild and breath-taking, and we savored it.

Kindergarten brought countless milestones and as many eye-openers regarding Genevieve's behaviors; they indicated how enormously challenged she was at surviving in a school environment. The morning of Halloween was a perfect example: I picked her up as usual, only to find her screaming and absolutely unglued! I was furious as I suspected that the staff had disregarded our warnings and had allowed her to have chocolate. But when I checked with the staff, that was not the case. Her reaction was purely one of extreme bombardment. It stood to reason. For a child with autism, the calmest of days at an elementary school can be bombarding; Halloween was over the top.

But if every dark cloud has a silver lining, the evening of that same Halloween brought an important breakthrough. Despite our efforts to separate her chocolaty loot when she was "trick-or-treating," Genevieve managed to sneak and devour some of the chocolate in her bag. By the time she arrived home, she was writhing in pain and torment, brought on by her severe reaction to chocolate. But it was the very first time that she could make the connection between eating a forbidden food and consequently, getting a severe reaction. She talked about it for days and it was a vital step in her understanding her body. And, she stopped asking for chocolate, even when she saw others with it.

Genevieve responded well to the structure and routine of the primary years at school and she made many casual friends, where she could flit in and out of their attention as she pleased. When she invited them home to play, it was a challenge. Sometimes it went well; sometimes it was a complete disaster. She would literally forget about her invited guest or tire of them. While she puttered around on her own, I was left in the precarious position of entertaining them while I scrambled to juggle Hayden. She did better when she visited her classmate's homes, as she wasn't as tempted to slip into the safety of her home refuge; how much she may have slipped into her own world when she was there, I could only imagine. "Brownies" was ideal because the social demands were minimal and there was enough structure and adult support to keep her more or less on track.

A "wild flower" and an "effervescent angel" were the terms that best described Genevieve, her world and her presence in it during the primary years. But the beauty of her world was constantly contradicted by her inability to deal with the realities of "our world". School was a daunting challenge and it was emotionally and physically exhausting for her to be exposed constantly to children and adults, hour after hour. In addition, there were the overwhelming sounds, scents and lighting present in the school. In grades one and two, when the school day was extended to a full six hours, she struggled even more.

Genevieve could manage "Show and Tell" types of conversations but couldn't tell about her personal experiences. If she was upset, she couldn't explain or describe how she felt or why she felt that way. Charts, stickers, rewards, incentives and "social stories" helped to shift her focus and prepare her for school activities, but they became a "drop in the bucket" in terms of addressing the level of anxiety that was growing.

At school, she often appeared to be happy and calm; yet once she got home, or simply saw the safety of "Mommy" at the end of the school day, she would fall apart at the seams. I found it hard to not take it personally, when staff would rave about her great school day; yet one look at me and she would be in pieces! It was terribly confusing to school staff and to me, because I could see and feel her agony; I knew it was real. And it was bitterly frustrating to me that teachers would get her best, as would family and friends when they would visit; then I'd be the one to glue her back together again afterwards.

I called this ungluing "aftershock". It became a part of her school life and her home life. She once, for instance, went with Sydney and Kobe, for a sleepover at the home of close family friends. She managed awesomely (she was pretty much wrapped up in her own little world for most of the visit); but when she came home, the place where she could let her guard down and be herself, she was completely unglued by the experience. She screamed, was argumentative, and was, at best, miserable to be with and at worst, wickedly temperamental. Genevieve paid, and we paid, a terrible price for five days afterward.

On schooldays, occasionally mornings went well. Many, many mornings, she would manage until the moment of transition from the car to the inside of the school. Then within seconds, she would be literally on her hands and knees, pleading and screaming at me not to leave her! One morning, the principal, a warm and caring man, reassured me that I just needed to be strong and ignore her outbursts. I looked back at him in disbelief and sheer frustration. He wasn't hearing and seeing in her what I could see, hear and feel. This was not a spoiled, manipulative child trying to get her way. She *wanted* to be a person who could go to school. She *wanted* to be able to handle all the things that she saw her peers handle. But she was tormented and affected right down to her soul. She was telling us that she couldn't manage in that environment, under those conditions.

Chapter 17

As a team, we had work to do. The many faces Genevieve wore at school and the extreme contrasts in her behavior between calm and tormented, dictated the need for us to overhaul and re-assess. The Amity staff had always embraced Genevieve with unwavering dedication; yet even in that knowledgeable and accepting environment, a mystery began to unravel, one that would take several years to fully understand and address. We called it "masking" and Genevieve was brilliant at it; she still is.

Throughout her life, masking has both opened doors for Genevieve, but has also closed them. Often she did not get the support and acknowledgement that she needed because her masking clouded and sometimes hid the pervasive impact of autism on her life. Masking has worked both *for* her and *against* her because it made it easy for people to forget and loose sight of how much she was affected and how hard she had to work to overcome her challenges. She has always been seen as an inspiration and a brave and courageous soul; but few really understand just how incredible she has been!

The masks that she would wear were as plain as day to me, but there were times when she had me guessing too. During the primary years, why did she often appear to have a good day at school and then go to pieces when she was at home, only to be on her hands and knees the next day at school, screaming like a caged animal and begging to go home? It was mystifying and often I took the blame, as if the problem was me being weak and giving in to her. But I could see and feel how deeply she was struggling. Many times over the years, I have exasperated myself and the people involved with her, trying to open up their eyes to see the implications of the masks that she wore and the reasons she felt the need to "wear" them. I could see it in her actions and in her body language; I could hear it in her voice and in her dialogue. But it was a formidable task in deciphering it and presenting it in terms that people could understand and act upon. That time would come.

But in the primary years, a gifted school psychologist did see Genevieve much through the perspective that I did; she too saw the masks. Her name was Sarah Maguire and she played such an important role in Genevieve's life and in our arduous journey. Very lovingly, and very insightfully (and very much to my relief), she referred to Genevieve as "the Queen of Deception". She didn't mean Genevieve was a manipulative child trying to take advantage of her "disability"; she meant quite the opposite. She saw an amazing child who used all of her powers to wear masks and not allow people to see how hard she worked, to face a world that her peers could prance through without missing a beat.

An unbelievable weight was lifted from my shoulders to have a partner, one within the school system, who shared this level of insight! But even for Sarah, deciphering Genevieve and putting into terms what she and I saw so clearly, was not an easy task. It was difficult to give teachers and therapists the tools that they needed to, in essence, give themselves "permission" to look beyond what they were seeing in front of them. We needed for them to read Genevieve's body language, her words and her actions so that they could grasp what Genevieve herself was telling us, and all that was really going on within her.

Sarah's insight was a true blessing. She and Genevieve had a very meaningful bond and though her involvement would only be for a few years, her presence altered the course of Genevieve's life. Sarah also affected people's understanding and appreciation for Genevieve's brilliance. Sarah Maguire was more than a gift to us; she was an angel and Genevieve and I still feel a happy glow at the mention of her name.

If Genevieve was, as Sarah and I both believed her to be, the Queen of Deception, she was also very much the Queen of Fantasy and the Queen of Artistic Interpretation. Like me, Sarah encouraged her to open up her kingdom and to *use* it to present herself to the world! We also guided her to continue doing what she had instinctively done for so long: to use it as a means of drawing the world *to* her. Over and beyond her own fulfillment and personal gain, we wanted Genevieve to give to the world, her passion for life and for things that were abstract, unique and beautiful. She had an amazing spin on life and we knew the world around her could only benefit from seeing it.

It was very curious and disconcerting to me, that the most prominent belief in dealing with autism meant that we should have been "squelching" that unique part of Genevieve's personality and her behaviors. Instead we should have been working on getting her head "out of the pink and fluffy clouds", and encouraging her to work and navigate in ways that were more tangible and more "typical". But what Sarah and I chose was to encourage Genevieve to do the opposite: to take her natural talents and personality to new heights and to use those "new heights" to increase her comfort level with the world and to ultimately understand the world.

With those goals in mind, Sarah quite stepped out of her usual capacity of school psychologist, a number of ways. She became the director of a thirty-page play that Genevieve wrote, based on the movie *The Pebble and the Penguin*. The children were very young for such an undertaking, only grade two; but Sarah, Genevieve and I worked along with the teacher for months, creating and rehearsing this important play. Genevieve even worked diligently with me at my sewing machine, making basic costumes for the cast. She learned immensely, as we all did. She blossomed and we were able to "slide in", without arousing her radar, something new and very important. It was the ability to be incredibly creative, but at the same time, keep her feet just a little bit on the ground. She learned to take control of her passion and tone it down a little, while still feeling proud and satisfied with her work.

For a play that had initially, in Genevieve's mind, the intent of encompassing a cast of thousands, with elaborate costumes and settings, she was able to slowly and cautiously, grasp and embrace the reality of keeping it to a small group of children, with reasonable props and expectations. This was a huge accomplishment that was far reaching in her development. *The Pebble and the Penguin* was a turning point and the successes went well beyond the applause she and her cast mates heard at the end of their little performance.

Later on in elementary school, Genevieve and I dreamed up another scheme: a Children's Theatre group. She and I could take classic movies or stories and re-write them to tailor-make roles for her and each of her school friends, who became the cast of each play. Always we would create some interesting twist to the story that made it our own and would captivate her friends. For months on end, the cast would come into our home, to learn scripts, make backdrops and rehearse. Each play was a huge undertaking but a delightful labor of love! Somehow, with Sydney, Kobe and Nolan's assistance, we pulled off several of them. Each was a fabulous endeavor and a way to allow Genevieve's classmates to see her where she was in her element and was most natural. And I was in my element, having the opportunity to be surrounded by children, scripts, paints, fabric and lots of chaos. Genevieve was always given free rein over the design and creation of programs for each play; she reveled in the glory of highlighting each cast member through her drawings and depictions and they all felt like stars!

We performed each play at a local church gym for friends and family to watch. To me there was nothing like seeing children have the opportunity to pull from within themselves courage and creativity, and the power to pretend. Our theatre group and our plays really were labors of love; but they were also *very* much strategic!

Chapter 18

In grade two, it was time to tell Genevieve about her autism. She was so bright, curious and perceptive and we knew that it was just a matter of time before she would overhear comments and put things together. We wanted her to hear it from us, in the terms that we had carefully chosen to use.

I can hardly describe how hard it was to remember and grab onto the words that I had rehearsed in my mind dozens of times. Where Nolan and I found our strength and our conviction was in knowing that they weren't simply words that we were telling her. They were what we genuinely saw in her: that her autism enormously challenged her but that she was more gifted than disabled. The challenge was in assisting her to understand her gifts and to deal with the drawbacks that those gifts imposed.

We did choose our words very carefully, to remove any link between her and Hayden or she would have been devastated. We explained that there were different forms of autism, some that lead to lack of speech and severe behavioral issues, as her brother presented. We told her that there was another form, much more rare, which is true, that gives "special powers" of imagination and creativity. We invited her to ponder: "Why else would her hearing be so acute? Why would her amazing artistic and literary talents have such a unique spin?" At first, she was a little confused, not knowing what to say or how to respond or if it was even true. Sydney jumped in soon afterward and gave words of invaluable support that only a child could have given.

We prayed that our timing was right. Panola, Genevieve's wonderful special ed assistant at the time, bought her a beautifully written and illustrated book called *Butterflies and Bottlecaps*. It was a captivating story about a little girl who was different because she had butterflies for hair. Though she felt happy with whom she was, she never really fit in until she discovered a little girl who had bottlecaps for hair. Genevieve connected immediately with the story and its vibrant images. We sent the book to school where her teacher shared it with the class. At the end of the reading, Genevieve stood up proudly and said: "I have autism". Later that night when I asked her about the discussion, she amazed me by explaining yet more about her "autism mind". I believe she has known since she was probably about age two that she was "different"; the book, our revelations about her autism and her "special powers" may have been like pieces of a puzzle coming together for her.

A few years later, the teacher of that time told me that Genevieve was "the most courageous student she had ever had", and she had taught for thirty-five years. I think our joint strategy was right and the timing was right. The sequence of events also highlighted the power of families and school staff, all working together!

Chapter 19

Throughout the first five or six years of elementary school we, as a team, utilized things that were safe and meaningful to Genevieve, often with very impressive results. It was amazing to witness how much mileage we could get using pink as her "comfort color". We taught her to "Think Pink" to feel more secure and to offer her a distraction from stressful situations. My heart told me so graphically that at school, she needed a safe haven, a precious little place that she could retreat to when she needed time to herself, to "escape reality" as she would later come to call it, or to use as a quiet place to work on her tougher assignments. Luckily, staff was receptive.

In a small, rarely-used classroom, a safe haven is exactly what Sydney and I crafted for Genevieve. It was a study carrol and every detail had to be perfect. We decorated it with adorable bunny wallpaper and pink tulle; I remember a tiny bird's nest with pastel eggs and there were two little exquisite, antique bunnies that I'd stumbled across in a little shop long before. I had tucked them away, knowing that one day their purpose would present itself. They found an important home on the shelf of the carrol. (I still have them today; I can't part with them).

The study carrol *did* make a difference. It was an important step in not only enabling Genevieve to feel safe; but to once again, acknowledge to her that we were all working together, navigating, each of us a part of this unique adventure. Even during the last year or two of elementary school, when Genevieve chose to no longer use the study carrol, she told me she wanted it left intact; she needed to know that it was still there.

Understanding Genevieve and embracing who she was opened the door to other tools. One, as simple as a pink placemat decorated with a happy face, could be slipped under her math worksheet, helping dramatically to reduce the stress of "dreaded math". Playful but potent social stories depicting Genevieve as a superhero fearlessly combating "The Horror of Math" also helped. One therapist, using cartoon drawings and witty captions, taught her to put a bubble over herself to concentrate and to feel protected from the school chaos around her.

These strategies were on Genevieve's wavelength and were very "Genevieve specific"; and she bought into them. Later, by grades six and seven, it was fascinating to see the way she signed her name on worksheets: it was always "Genevieve the_____" (something witty that she used to describe herself; and each time it was something different). Less insightful teachers might have demanded that she stop, interpreting her as being impertinent; but what we could all see she was doing, was that she was skillfully making herself a *part* of that worksheet, so that she could then feel safe enough, to then focus on her work.

Much of the success was two-fold. These social stories, their characters and our subtle "props" fulfilled Genevieve's need to have a non-human "buffer" between her and the source of anxiety. I think it went deeper: it also came back to the importance of her feeling that we were acknowledging that these were very real issues and real challenges for her and that we were "meeting her halfway". We were doing it with respect, sensitivity and her brand of mature wit!

In addition to the color pink, zebra stripes and zebras as an animal, have also offered immeasurable inspiration and security. She and I have called upon them countless times over the years in a multitude of ways, for powerful visualizations and meditations and strategies, focusing not only on the visual appearance of the stripes, but the furry sensation that she links with her favorite animal. Likely her love affair began back in grade one, when she created her first little book series about "Zena the Zebra". As behavioral strategies or items to collect for her room or to wear, Genevieve learned to "wrap herself up" in pink or in zebra stripes or even better, in both.

At school, there was always a fine line between treating Genevieve like a typical child and one with autism. She didn't want to be hovered over, but very much wanted to know that the support was there if and when she needed it. As a team, we worked together to soul search, to ponder and explore Genevieve's behaviors and reactions to things at school. It was essential that I worked closely with each team member, every step of the way, to orchestrate, constantly pulling things together and making adjustments. I documented and re-evaluated our successes and failures.

The aftershock that we dealt with was indeed, a part of Genevieve's "masking". On the outside, it often appeared that she could handle a day of school, and yet she would fall apart at the end of it. Sarah Maguire was one of the few people who could give credibility to what we were piecing together at home. She could see and express to staff that it took so much out of Genevieve, physically and emotionally to get through the day, that the moment the school day was over, she was completely used up. There simply was nothing left, and so she went to pieces and lashed out at the world and most specifically, at her family. Often during the primary years, Genevieve refused to sleep alone and crawled in with Sydney which was very uncharacteristic of her. On some of the roughest nights, out of concern and compassion, Kobe would crawl in as well, to offer his support. It was very, very sweet but was certainly an indicator that she was deeply struggling to be at school.

As parents, we encouraged the school staff to take Genevieve's lead when dealing with aftershock issues. She was notorious for managing well during the chaos of field trips only to crash and be unable to face school the next day. No doubt for many people, especially those not trained in autism, she appeared to be a highly manipulative child on the surface; but you only had to stand back and look at the broader spectrum of her behaviors to realize what she was really doing. She was not lazy and manipulative; she was working and learning how to enable herself to survive. That was proven time and time again, after each field trip. Home she would stay, snuggled up in our big bed, with all of her stuffed animal friends, taking in Disney movies. It was very clear to us at home that she was willfully retreating and lapping up, almost overdosing, in the security, familiarity and vibrancy of her beautiful world. By the following day, she would be ready and more than willing to head back to school.

One of the driving forces behind writing this book has been to acknowledge and celebrate Genevieve's sincerity and determination, and her brilliance in finding ways to navigate. Never, ever has she taken advantage or asked for more than she needed. Even at the age of seven, she knew herself well enough to know to pull back, recharge and then get back into life the moment she felt she could. This is an incredible ability for an adult, much less a child.

When faced with bigger events like returning to school after Spring Break, Genevieve navigated her way back by returning completely in character. She scripted herself with specific clothes, make-up and a unique hairstyle; one year, she even spoke with an accent and used an assumed name. She was not simply pretending. She was embracing the formidable challenge of returning to school after a break, and she was very serious. She was both crushed and furious, if anyone strayed from her "script" and called her Genevieve. She wasn't playing; she *was* that character. She needed to be that character.

Gradually, as years passed, she managed with less-dramatic disguises, to the point where she sometimes needed only her reading glasses for the first day back. To this day, she continues to skillfully use bits of accessories and how she postures herself and her presence, to take steps that are challenging and sometimes unnatural to her. Her life and her "tale" have been very much on-going depictions of the human spirit!

With respect to children with autism and being in school, there is one thing that has always mystified me. I've pondered and questioned it countless times with my own two children and with others I have seen, and with the ones I have had the privilege of working with. It is this: any insightful parent of an autistic child learns early on that these children simply cannot be in their family's presence all of the time. They need breaks, time to be on their own to process and to deal with the world around them. Even in the most loving and conducive home, I am betting that is the case for most, if not all. Why is it that we put them in a school and think that they will magically be able to function, hour after hour, for a total of six hours, in a sensory and socially bombarding environment that far exceeds anything they would experience in their own home?

It just doesn't make sense. For most, perhaps for all, especially in the younger years, it is unrealistic and in my view, disrespectful. I've seen the damage done when this need is not honored (and not only with my own children); but I've also seen the *real magic* that happens when it is creatively and insightfully addressed!

Chapter 20

Genevieve's creative soul, her imaginative powers, and the way that we carefully cultivated them throughout her life, have indeed made her journey unique. I am aware that imagination and creativity do not come intrinsically to all children and adults on the autism spectrum. For some, it is not easily cultivated nor is it the route to follow. Every child with autism is unique; that is part of the reason why it is such a difficult disorder to address. *Effervescence*, the tale about this particular child, is not meant to be a blanket roadmap that can be transferred to fit the needs of any child on the spectrum. My hope is that you will interpret it more as book of "paintings and illustrations" that will help you enter the mind and the body of autism; though each child and adult is unique, there are many, many common threads that connect them. *Effervescence* is also intended as an illustration of the power and importance for us "outsiders" to be relentless and creative in finding ways in, into their hearts and into their unique world, no matter how far we might have to step out of our own world to do it.

I remember an "autism mom" I met many years ago. She was understandably woeful, because her family was not having much success in reaching her young autistic son. My heart went out to her and to her son; but it was curious to me and it stuck with me all these years, when she made the comment that her son really didn't have anything in his life that he connected deeply with, other than electrical diagrams. It seemed sad to me that she didn't seem excited or motivated by that. As the words left her lips, I found myself wondering: "Wow, maybe that's where she should be grabbing! Why is she not wearing dresses and t-shirts with electrical diagrams splattered all over them?" Maybe it wouldn't have moved mountains; maybe it wouldn't have done anything at all, but at least it would have been a hopeful attempt. Or maybe it *would* have opened some little door between her and her son.

I don't pretend to have all the answers because each child is so unique; but if he were my son, that's where I would have started. If stepping back, looking through his eyes at what was safe and meaningful to him, meant letting him visually see and feel those electrical diagrams all over me, I would have been hand painting dresses and t-shirts myself! For this young boy, Fantasy would not have been the way "in" as it was for Genevieve; but there had to be something. Maybe they just hadn't found it yet.

Chapter 21

From early childhood and through the elementary school years, reprimand was ineffectual and often harmful to Genevieve. She basically shut down in response. Her life was very much governed by rule-based behavior and rules enabled her to pace herself and feel structure that was safe and gave her a sense of control over the chaos that surrounded her. Being reprimanded meant that she had broken the rules and she took it very seriously and very personally.

She set high standards for herself and would crumble if she felt that people around her had thought that she had not met them. In younger years, a negative or stern remark, even a casual one from a teacher, was enough to shatter her confidence and self-esteem for weeks. She still shutters at the thought of a substitute teacher back in grade two, who told her to "smarten up". It was devastating and she couldn't face school for three weeks afterward. It still has a haunting affect on her.

That little incident was an eye opener and a mixed blessing. It proved to staff how fragile she was and why. It was a reminder that despite all the "masks" that Genevieve wore and all of her little survival skills, she was affected much more pervasively than most people were able and willing to admit. In response, we all worked to carefully and creatively increase her ability to safeguard herself from the potency of such comments. For children with autism, there really is a nebulous division between rules giving structure and rules bombarding.

The rules and procedures within the classroom, offered many double-edged swords between being helpful and being a force that could push Genevieve over the edge. In learning, we found that once she was taught a skill or a process, she considered it to be carved in stone. If a teacher tried to teach it or present it in a different way at a later date it invoked rigidness, often lead to a shut down, and always caused a temperamental outburst or meltdown.

On the lighter side, some of Genevieve's interpretation of rules and her need to comply, was just plain cute! If we tried to whisper to her in a movie theatre or even worse of a crime, try to wave to her when she was onstage for a Christmas concert at school, she would dart "daggers" back at us because in her mind, the rule was that we should all be quiet, attentive and unassuming.

Drawing became another powerful stepping stone for Genevieve. Though her early drawings were rudimentary, there was always some tiny detail that made her creations unique and different from what her peers would have drawn. Even then, it was obvious that she took in miniscule details in everyday life that the rest of us took very much for granted, and she experienced them on a different level. She instinctively knew how to put genuine personality into her characters. It might have been a tiny detail, like a clock or a bottle of perfume. It might have been merely buttons on a tuxedo or a wink, or even a single eyelash, much less a look in a character's eye! These "tiny" details made her drawings unique and enabled her personality and her uncanny insight to shine through.

Always family and friends were depicted by Genevieve, as animal characters. We assumed it was because that was where she felt safest. By grade one, she wrote short "novels" that showcased not only her flair for writing, illustrating and creating unique story lines but also her ability and need to be social *through* her creations. At school she mastered her "Zena the Zebra" novels and each one was about ten pages long. That was an impressive undertaking for any six-year-old; and these novels meant the world to her! When she was finally able to bring them home from school, she was so thrilled and overcome with gladness that the night before, she woke me up at 3:00am. She was determined to find and decorate a box, not simply to store her novels in but, I suspected, to give them a "home" of their own. Her entire body, in the middle of the night, was bursting with pride and eager anticipation as we transformed a Ritz cracker box. The fact that her family was finally going to be able to see her novel creations appeared to be of secondary importance to her, if anywhere in her thoughts at all. Her characters and her stories were so incredibly real to her, that her excitement was all about bringing her precious friends into her home to live, along with her.

She still has that box of self-written novels. Though she now writes with great skill and maturity that surpasses any of our expectations back when she was six, she occasionally re-reads her Zena novels, like re-visiting old friends. She likes to know that that part of her history is still there, amongst all of her treasures.

During the primary and intermediate school years, Genevieve was a bottomless well of artistic energy, talent and insight. I've saved hundreds of drawings and creations and still marvel, as each of them is an exploration of human nature and day-to-day endeavors. There are stories and tiny novels about Romance, Fantasy and even Terror. One of them was entitled "Genevieve's Three Haunting Tales of Terror"; her cartoon-type illustrations were "dripping in blood" and were amazing, especially considering she was still only a primary-aged child. She wrote little period pieces like "The Duchess and the Demon" in which all of her characters were drawn in medieval costumes with startling accuracy. All of the details were strictly from memory, taken from little bits of things she'd seen in movies or in print, but never copied directly from a book or a picture. She had an amazing ability to see an object, sometimes for only a brief moment, and later draw it, recapturing many of the details.

At the very young age of seven or eight, Genevieve was creating posters and "Question and Answer" cards about her favorite characters, intended for her family and friends to answer. She made paper dolls with clothes and paper tabs to attach them. She created actual newspapers with witty and insightful articles, bubble captions and pictures. The list went on and on. In her writing, her emotions and responses had a noticeable, unfiltered quality to them. Some were intensely humorous and bitingly witty and satirical, like her novella entitled "Our Deepest Fears". It was set in the year 2019 when all chocolate factories would close and all radio stations would have to play the music of Jewel, non-stop.

Genevieve made board games with intricate rules. Some were simple but utterly fascinating, intended only for her personal use and enjoyment. My favorite was called "Picking a Boyfriend". It was based on "Pin the Tail on the Donkey" and involved a poster she created with drawings of several boys from her class, in particular, Aidan who was the love of her life. She attached it to a wall, and I would find her blind-folded, spinning in circles, arm outstretched and ready to "pick a boyfriend". She'd play it over and over and it was very interesting how often she could, in her blind-folded stupor, always seem to find Aidan.

Genevieve wrote touching stories, some based on classics but with her own personal and witty twist. Even Sydney and Kobe, at their young ages, were amazed and delighted by the depth of her creativity. She focused vast amounts of her time and energy on entertaining her family. She dreamed up countless skits for us to watch or be a part of. When she started learning math, she made unbelievable math drills for Sydney, Kobe and even Hayden; each one age appropriate, in the sense that Hayden had simple 1+1 questions, Kobe's were tougher and Sydney's were the toughest. Each always had a section at the bottom with a maze, a witty puzzle or a drawing activity.

And much to our exasperation, there were polls, endless polls for us to answer, surveying every imaginable topic! They were not random activities to Genevieve; what she was doing, was studying "us". She was learning about people and she was letting us into her world, into her thoughts and her unique way of thought processing. As a family, we were exasperated and exhausted. We were ready to pull our hair out at the prospect of another poll; but we were *equally* fascinated!

At school, Genevieve saw her classmates the way she saw her family: as an entity, like they were characters in the play that was her life. At the age of seven, when she was still very much struggling to feel physically and socially comfortable at school (and everywhere for that matter), she told me about an actual dream she'd had, in which each class member was an animal toy. She listed off all twenty-one in detail. She was obsessive about the dream and I could see that this was not something to be taken lightly. She was striving to find ways of making these people who were in her life, safe to actually *be* in her life.

In response to her dream, she then carefully handpicked twenty-one of her animal figurines to represent each student, depending on their appearance and personality type. I was captivated because I could see that her strategy was that through her animal figurines, her classmates could then be physically *with her* in the safe haven of her bedroom. She could then, in essence, "try them on for size" and get used to them and their presence in her life. Through her solitary play, she was actually building relationships with each individual classmate. Gradually, her relationship with each animal figurine/classmate, carried over into the outside world and her comfort level and ability to socialize with them increased. I was in awe of her brilliance and her determination!

Through her drawings, Genevieve mentally prepared herself for upcoming issues and events in her life. Some of that she learned from us and from therapists, as these drawings were an extension of "social stories". But she took the concept to much deeper and more complex levels. For example, at the age of eight, I found pictures she had drawn of herself with Sydney's ballet teacher. Though she had only seen the instructor a few times, she drew with intriguing detail. What she had done, all on her own, was a drawing to see how it would "feel" to take ballet. What an amazing skill! For years after, I would peruse through her drawings whenever I saw a stack, so that I could take a peak inside her head and check up on what might be troubling, challenging or baffling her.

It was through one of her private stacks of drawings that I realized she was conscious of being a little bit chubby and that some of the kids at school had been making fun of her. I found a dozen drawings of *Sailor Moon* characters, drawn sequentially from thin to heavier, the last being quite chubby. It nearly broke my heart to find her pictures but I was grateful that she had found a way of acknowledging and exploring feelings that she couldn't grasp and put into words. Without referring to her pictures or letting her in on the fact that I had seen them, I was able to subtly chip away at the issue of weight and of body image.

Genevieve's drawings and her countless little animal figurines, were not just characters and toys; they were her lifeline. She knew each of her animal figurines by the species and by the name and personality traits that she assigned to them. Like the characters in her drawings, they were a very real and essential part of her life. They certainly were as real as any living creature or person. I thought it was a terrible injustice not to acknowledge their power and potential. They were not simply toys or a child's "doodlings". *They were soul- searching explorations of a very intelligent, sensitive and gifted individual who was very much in touch with her own strengths and weaknesses, even at the ripe old age of eight.* Much of Genevieve's work and her musings were very self-absorbed but packed with humor, like her caricatures of herself in "The Unlikely Professions of Genevieve". In these drawings, she humorously and insightfully perused the occupations that would highlight her weaknesses.

Genevieve's sense of humor and sparkle underlay all of her creations, whether they were original stories or parodies that she based on other works. They were packed with energy, enthusiasm and her unique "worldliness" that was well beyond her years.

A few years ago, Genevieve and I were deep in a conversation where she expressed the amazing realization that much of her struggle to feel comfortable around her peers wasn't simply *because* of her autism and because she was an artist; it was a direct result of the insight and perspective she had gained because of her autism. She said when it was lunchtime at school and she was trying to hang out with her peers, listening to their conversation and the way they handled themselves, made her feel like she was "fifteen going on thirty".

Having autism gave her a vantage point that she wouldn't have otherwise had. She had a level of perceptiveness that was oddly staggering, almost alarming. And because she lacked "social filters", she had the courage to present them in her unabashed and creative ways. That had started way back; it's what came out in her early drawings and compositions.

Chapter 22

The issue of physical contact was confusing. All the literature at the time described autistic children as being repelled by it. But it certainly wasn't what we saw consistently in Genevieve, nor in Hayden. It wasn't that she didn't want physical contact; it seemed more that if she got it, she didn't always know how to respond to it. She seemed to desire it for different reasons than we did, and she accepted it on terms that were different than ours'. Since birth, Genevieve was often very snuggly with me, and sometimes with her dad, but it felt "different" than it did with the other kids; it was very much on a deep, sensory level. Throughout the elementary years, she often craved physical contact and pressure. She loved for us to sit on her with our entire body weight pressing against her. And she was most comfortable seeking out physical contact with her feet and even her legs, often incessantly. Even into her teens she would sweetly hold my hands, and sometimes those of her dad's, stroking and tapping them, like she was repelled yet drawn and needy all at the same time. She often made the observation that "kisses were yucky and hugs were too squishy".

I was surprised, even at the age of eight, how often Genevieve still wanted me to pick her up and hold her. At Kobe's baseball barbeque, I was met with a lot of strange looks as I carried her, at her request, much as I would have carried a toddler. Honestly, I didn't care; all I had to do was remind myself of the countless times that she had pushed me away. Trust me; when you have an autistic child and they indicate that they want to be held, and they are willing to wrap themselves around you, you make the whole world stop. You drop everything and enjoy it. And in the case of this particular social event, Genevieve needed to make herself feel safe because of the social overload. And to me, holding my eight-year-old child was certainly better than dealing with the alternative that had ruined so many social events in the past, when she had pushed us away, tuned us out and retreated to screaming and spinning in circles!

One of my greatest fears and regrets about Genevieve's unusual behaviors was that she would be misinterpreted as being spoiled, belligerent, manipulative and self-serving. From an outside, misinformed perspective, her determination, passion and struggle to survive could have been interpreted that way. Autism does not have physical characteristics, unlike for instance, Down syndrome. It is a blessing but it can work against a child, or adult: because they do not look "different", onlookers may not realize that they have a disability and will then misinterpret their behaviors and respond as though it is simply a matter of a character flaw or choice.

Chapter 23

Despite her many elementary school successes, by grade five Genevieve expressed emphatically to me, that she saw "home as a garden and school as a prison". That was the year she crashed. She crumbled; she lashed out and she went to pieces. She refers to it now as her "breakdown year" and still shudders at the memory of it.

Grade five had been a terribly stressful school year and the concept of "masking" was rampant. Often Genevieve would manage relatively well at school, only to be an absolute mess when she got home. I would casually ask how her day went, only to be blasted with screaming and sometimes hysterical ranting of: "I don't know, I don't know, I don't want to talk about it, I don't have to talk about it…" She flapped her hands wildly, talking rapidly and obsessively about "Bart Simpson this and Homer Simpson that". Often after school, not a single word that came out of her mouth was *not* Simpson related. I was distraught because I recognized the signs: in order to survive, she was tuning into her safe world, on a level that was extremely alarming!

At home we were gravely concerned because she was falling apart at the seams. Even her ability to accept the foods that she had traditionally considered to be "safe" was affected. She became mistrusting of the foods that we offered her, that normally she would have welcomed. Her tolerance of Hayden dropped dramatically. It made a sharp and important contrast to her relationship with him the previous summer, when we had rejoiced to see an unprecedented improvement in her willingness and ability to be in his presence. That indicated to us that Hayden was not at the root of the current problem, as school staff were claiming.

What followed was a domino effect. Hayden was seriously thrown by Genevieve's stressful behaviors, as were Sydney and Kobe; that in turn, severely affected Nolan and me. Once again, life in our home became unbearable. It was on the most serious level we had experienced in several years and we found ourselves thrust amidst a terribly complex situation. We knew our family could not endure another relapse into ridiculous levels of stress and chaos; but things were snowballing quickly and soon, we weren't heading there, we were there.

Though we were working with school staff that we loved and had cultivated long-term relationships with, they weren't listening and they certainly weren't allowing themselves to see what was going on.

What was going on? To some degree, we were relieved to see that this crisis was not a direct result of the stress inflicted on Genevieve by her brother. Fueled by that knowledge, we delved into every aspect of Genevieve's life, particularly her time at school and the ripple effects that each daily experience was causing. It was a complex picture. She loved her peers and the concept of going to school and of learning and evolving; but at the best of times, the school environment was mentally and physically exhausting for her; it always had been. Now the gap was growing between her and the other children, socially and academically. Her difficulty in socializing naturally, particularly with the girls, was heightened by her refusal to "conform" as was typical for girls that age. She referred to them as sheep and she was deeply resentful of them.

In their defense each of her classmates was struggling to find their own way in their pre-teen confusion, and her obvious disapproval of their conforming ways widened the gap dramatically. In her eyes it was her worst nightmare, to see them succumbing to what she considered to be sad and unacceptable levels of conformity. They dressed alike, they spoke the same and they shunned anyone who dared to not be like them. It cut her to the core because it went against everything she believed in. The reality was, it wasn't just that she was autistic; she was a writer and an artist and always, her individuality and uniqueness were at the centre of her being. It was what had driven her and motivated her to climb all the mountains she had somehow found ways to tackle. It had *never* been a goal for her, to duplicate her peers or be just like them. Her goals had been to become enough like them that she could fit into their lives and reciprocate in ways that were safe and meaningful to her, and to also, offer to them, who she was. In earlier years, they had been receptive and embracing, but now that was changing.

Genevieve's peers were growing less tolerant and understanding of her "quirks" and her obsessions. In all fairness to them, she wasn't always easy to get along with. She could be terribly opinionated and outspoken about her interests and the things that were precious to her. Because she had autism, she lacked the "filters" that would have otherwise enabled her to express herself more sensitively. She had little if any, ability to see the perspective of anyone but herself. Most of these kids had been with her since kindergarten and they had had enough of tiptoeing around her, trying not to upset or offend her.

Genevieve's fixations and obsessions stemmed, of course, from more than just her genuine interest. She purposely and intuitively used them as a vehicle to bridge the gap between herself and the others. She knew that she needed them if she was to survive and navigate throughout her classroom and the school. It was a vicious circle because now that school was an increasing source of stress and anxiety, she clung to her fixations and obsessions even more; that made things worse. Not surprisingly, her passion for the Spice Girls was dangerously threatened by the increasing popularity of *Pokemon* and she feared that they would overtake the presiding role of the Spice Girls within the school community. She literally feared "what would be left of her without them".

She expressed to me many times that she felt very alone, particularly at recess and lunch. She complained that everyone treated her "like a criminal". Sunday evenings become increasingly rough and we'd watch her unravel at the prospect of a new school week starting the next day. She was able to articulate to me how depressed and "not herself" she was each Sunday evening.

We worked on skills and incentives to associate Sundays more positively. Genevieve told me how she herself had taken to meditating in the traditional yoga pose and could see herself flying around the world. She liked doing it at school, but complained that it didn't work well there because of the noise. It was best in her bedroom where it was quiet. In the school playground, the swings were her reprieve, where she went to "escape reality". Sometimes her "feeling alone and like a criminal" was from her own point of view, and because she felt them so physically and intensely, it stopped her from seeing the moments when her classmates were inclusive and friendly. She wasn't able to see it and it tormented her.

But the harsh reality definitely was there; it wasn't all in her head. Many of Genevieve's friends and classmates did turn on her. Some maliciously ridiculed her about her obsessions with things like the Spice Girls. They knew her well enough to know how to push her buttons and they were pushing them and watching her crumble. There were incidents where she was so distraught that she actually responded by frantically kicking them, out in the playground. Never before had she behaved this way at school!

As parents, we were not told of these incidents. We found out through Kobe, who was of course, extremely upset and concerned. Amongst the staff, there seemed to be a new shroud of secrecy that revealed to Nolan and myself that we and the staff were no longer working as a team, the way we had since kindergarten.

To this day, I don't really understand why this issue was not addressed in our "tried and true" method, of working together, all on the same page. This was a staff of dedicated, talented and accommodating teachers and assistants; it made no sense to us and was deeply frustrating and alarming. I'm not so sure if it was that they were trying to keep it from us or that they just really didn't understand how serious an indicator of

Genevieve's stress level these incidents were. But how could they have not known? For months, I had reported to them our concerns from what we were seeing at home, and that was without knowing about her physically lashing out at classmates at school.

Sheila, Genevieve's special ed assistant who had worked with her for a number of years, still insisted that school was, for Genevieve, a safe haven. What Sheila wasn't letting herself see was that *she* was Genevieve's safe haven, not the school.

Perhaps as staff, they felt Genevieve's outbursts at school were a school issue and therefore should have been dealt with simply at the school level; and to their credit, they did effectively tackle some of the difficulties that Genevieve's peers were having in understanding her. But it wasn't enough; there was still so much that they were not seeing. As parents, we should have been kept in the loop, as should have been our behavioral therapist and psychologist. She was a complex child and that team connection was imperative.

The staff was too quick to blame Genevieve's aggressive outbursts and meltdowns on the impact of Hayden. It signified that they did not see the importance of looking at the whole picture. And they did not acknowledge what was coming out of Genevieve's own mouth and heart as to what the problems were. They didn't seem to be able to make the connection that the incessant "Simpson's jargon" at home, was in itself a sign of the severity of what was going on.

I had spent years documenting and analyzing her behavior and I knew how to "get in her head" and yet I wasn't taken seriously. Genevieve was not a child who was typically aggressive, at least not since her younger years when the world was a very different place to her. The fact that she had now resorted to those kinds of behaviors indicated that the underlying school stress had been smoldering away within her for a long time. The fact that it had come to such a head was indicative of her superb masking skills but also indicative of the staff's inability to read her and acknowledge the magnitude of the issues and the consequent behaviors.

At home, we had seen the smoldering and were forced to watch it grow to a height where it did blow and could then not be denied. This *was* a breakdown. This effervescent angel was not floating amongst soft and fluffy pink clouds, passing from "her world to ours"; she had crashed. There were moments, sometimes even days, when she could present herself to the world and appear to be functioning; but she *had* crashed and we were not about to let it continue.

Chapter 24

$\mathcal{I}$ do believe that part of the problem that lead to Genevieve's breakdown, was that the school staff didn't want to open their eyes to the fact that other children were acting maliciously towards her. The reality was that even in that conducive and cultivated school community, not all children responded compassionately. The fact that Genevieve lived in a home with a highly volatile autistic brother made it all too easy to attribute the seriousness of her behaviors to him.

The signs were there and they had to be recognized. She was falling apart at the seams, at home and often at school; yet staff continued to downplay it. I knew that if I were to watch Genevieve at school, I would have seen as they did, many heart-warming examples of Genevieve doing well, enjoying her friends and her work. But I also knew that I would see what the staff was not seeing: a brilliant actress hard at work. I would know by the tone in her voice, by her dialogue, her choice of words and the way that she carried herself at school. I was exasperated. Did she need to be spinning in circles, crowing and screaming, as she did before she learned her coping skills, to raise the staff's concern?

I wondered if her teachers really understood how Genevieve lived. What they saw at school was not what her life was like outside of nine to three. In order to survive those hours and to recover from them, she needed enormous amounts of solitary time, where she could tune out the world and replenish, physically and emotionally. She paid such high prices. Much of the reason she had the strength to get through each school day was because she knew she could return to her home, lock her bedroom door and slip into her wonderful, safe haven. That had been her reality and her way of life when things were going well and she was feeling at peace, accepted and not too overwhelmed by the academic and social expectations. Imagine what it had been like, month after month when she was feeling unaccepted and "like a criminal" at school?

There was also, within the school, a noticeable shift in the mandate which came from the new liaison support teacher, Mrs. Perry. Sarah Maguire was now gone, as were the liaison teachers of the earlier years, who had embraced the creative strategies that had worked so well. Now the goal was one of "guiding", of almost coercing Genevieve to act and respond the way her typical peers did; and we were to tackle her learning issues with very rigid, conventional and generic approaches. *It was a dramatic contrast from what we had proven to be so successful.* As parents, we perceived it as overtly squelching who Genevieve was, of what came naturally to her and what utilized her strengths and gifts. This was not acceptable. It was counter-productive and damaging. It was disrespectful to Genevieve. She had spent her entire young life exemplifying to the world that she knew she was different, that she knew she had to find ways to adapt; but that what mattered the most to her, was that she had the right to maintain what she felt was her intrinsic need to be unique and to be someone she felt proud of.

As parents and as a family, we could still feel the genuine warmth from the Amity staff that we had always felt; but there was a wall dividing us and it was even more pronounced by the allegiance they felt to support the concepts of the new liaison teacher. Though it was very foreign to us, we had no choice but to push the issue and make it very clear that things were not going to continue in this direction. But it wasn't just a matter of addressing the programming and the behavioral strategies; it was equally a matter of opening their eyes, so they could see what they were not seeing.

We demanded a team meeting and for the very first time ever, we included all levels of staff involved, right up to the principal and the Director of Special Programs for the district. As distraught as we were, we stayed clear of making it an opportunity to outright reprimand or blame. Yes, we were angry and frustrated by the staff's reluctance to listen to our concerns. And we were furious by Mrs. Perry and her painfully traditional and damaging perspective; but why would we have wasted precious energy in such a negative and counter-productive way? It really wasn't in Nolan's nature, or in mine. As resentful as I was, having had this woman stare back at me on many occasions and openly disregard the kinds of strategies and perspectives that had worked well with Genevieve in the past, I still felt some level of compassion for her because there really were few roadmaps to follow with these kids. They are extraordinarily complex and in this case, I think Mrs. Perry was very much out of her league. She had that very short-sighted perspective on autism that unfortunately so many people in this field have. Our equally exasperating encounters with her and Hayden's progress at school made that very clear.

Our goal in meeting, was more to engage each of the people involved, to let them see Genevieve on a level that they hadn't until now, either because she had masked it, or because they just didn't have the expertise in autism to really comprehend it. The hope and the force that drove us, was to firmly but creatively open their eyes in a way that would entice them to *want* to work on a higher and more insightful level. That would be a tall order.

As fate would have it, just two weeks prior to our team meeting, I had the opportunity to meet with a unique agency operated by a small group of autistic adults. As I sat back and listened to the presentation, I was moved so deeply to realize that nothing they said came as a shock to me. In fact, it was like finding the missing pieces to a puzzle that I had been working so arduously to complete. It was not a light presentation. Each member spoke candidly about his/her life experiences, about efforts to fit in, to try to be molded and then the subsequent challenges and turmoil. Several talked about years of depression and even attempts at suicide. It was alarming but I felt such a strong connection with each of them. I felt incredibly empowered and relieved to hear that from their perspective, the road that I had instinctively followed in working with both of my autistic children was right on. That was insight and confirmation that I needed to get, not from teachers or therapists, but from living and breathing adults with autism.

Preparation for the team meeting was not joyful. It meant weeks of compiling complex information, of sifting through past family traumas and opening up details of our history. We wanted to make our requests, our concepts and philosophies heartfelt but not overwhelming. The toughest part was being acutely aware how much was at stake. If staff and the school board did not buy into it, we knew we had a very difficult and treacherous road ahead of us. Genevieve was hardly keeping herself together; our family was once again in a serious crisis situation. Both Nolan and I were pushed far beyond what could have been remotely considered a survivable amount of stress. But what this meeting *did* offer us was an opportunity for each staff member's undivided attention, and an opportunity to draw them in.

I won't lie and say that in my presentation, I wasn't able to get in a few subtle digs as to the impact of Mrs. Perry's perspective; but I think she was probably surprised and relieved to see that anything beyond that was not our purpose or intention. With the full support of our insightful psychologist, Dr. Bryson, we were successful in presenting our two goals. First, we painted graphic but meaningful pictures of Genevieve to impress upon them the reality that she was much more challenged and complex than they had previously been aware. Second, we carefully indicated that "pounding a square peg into a round hole" was stomping and stifling the creative soul that was Genevieve and was indeed, damaging. We were not going to stand back and watch it continue to happen. We stressed that it was counter-productive to the wealth of creative strategies and concepts, that were at our fingertips if we all, as a team, embraced who Genevieve was.

The meeting was a huge success and we felt that for the first time, Genevieve's "complexities" were recognized and acknowledged. We did pull together as a team, with each person offering their little "piece of Genevieve", through their experiences and interpretations in working with her. I think each of the staff had to do a little soul searching and come to terms with some of the harsh realities, that academically and socially, they had been a little unrealistic and overly-optimistic. They hadn't been seeing the whole picture or looking behind the masks; they really hadn't been acknowledging that the masks were indeed masks.

The changes that resulted from that meeting were important; some were subtle and abstract, some were very tangible and concrete. What was most important, and what had been my foremost goal, was to open the staff's eyes so that they could "read" Genevieve better, to see the signs that they had been missing or misinterpreting. We modified some of her classes, acknowledging that she needed more time to herself to recharge and to recover from the physical and social stimuli that abounded throughout the classroom and the school itself. Also acknowledged was the need for more subtle support with activities, especially those with rules and procedures. Also it was recognized that she needed more casual support with her interactions amongst peers, and always time to herself afterward to "compensate".

Genevieve's physical signs of stress and discomfort were explored more by staff, so that they could offer her gentle and unobtrusive support. Some of her physical signs were subtle, like scratching her head or getting red in the face when she was feeling overwhelmed. Some were to us as parents, very obvious, like the alarming overuse of "Simpson's jargon" or talking to imaginary characters. As a team, we all worked with renewed conviction and greater awareness, and with a common vision. And what was left most intact, was our "predecessor", the concept of working *along* with Genevieve's creative being and tapping into those capabilities, as opposed to fighting them and trying to squelch them.

As for the children who had been mistreating Genevieve: they were dealt with, not so much with reprimand but with insight and support.

Genevieve quickly saw that the climate on all levels of school was changing. Her sense of inner peace gradually increased. We saw it both at home and at school and it was a very important turning point. Something else that I could read all over her body was that she could recognize that once again, we were "meeting her halfway". She didn't want sympathy or patronizing; she'd never, *ever* asked for that. All she wanted was support and insightfulness as to all the little complex threads that wove together to make the unique person that she was.

Chapter 25

Grades six and seven saw many ups and downs; but much was happy, productive and fascinating! At school there was noticeably more harmony amongst Genevieve and her peers. And the world around her continued to be as much mesmerized by her, as baffled. She was so curiously bright and insightful, with perspective about human nature that was well beyond her years; that came through more and more in her writing and illustrations. Yet it was perturbing how she struggled socially. She was often unable to carry her insights and perspectives into her own real social situations and interactions. Despite her amazing bravery, the reality was that she had autism and what should have been simple conversations for a child her age, were not simple at all. They did not come naturally or instinctively. She had a *body* that had autism; often even when she did figure things out, she perceived things on an extraordinarily sensory level which always complicated the interaction.

The sensory component of autism is very difficult to understand, much less to explain and it varies uniquely from one autistic individual to another. In my experience with my own two children and with others that I have worked with, I have found this component to be very much overlooked and consequently not addressed or taken into account, when dealing with their behaviors. Maybe it's another one of those complex issues where you really need to live very much "submerged, 24/7" in autism before you really start to "get it".

But with her zest for learning ever intact, Genevieve continued to learn, and inch by inch, she tested the social waters. At home, she wrote intricate scripts that were sharp and witty, which she would act out for us with her Barbie dolls. She would work, quite obsessively for weeks prior, preparing the tiniest of details in her script and with the backdrops and movie sets that she created. She made movie tickets for us and on the night of a performance, it meant the world to her that we would be her audience and video tape the performance.

Her performances, her "movies", were fascinating but demanding and complex for those of us in her audience. After each show and for days afterward, she would ask us detailed questions about the current movie as well as her past movie plots, scenes and characters. She expected that we would remember and give our opinions and predictions as to their longevity within her movie career. One Saturday evening, Genevieve hosted her own "People's Choice Awards Night". She created detailed ballots about the various categories from the many "movies" she had written and produced. As a family and as her captive audience, we were torn between being fascinated and tremendously grateful that she was letting us into her world, and being absolutely exasperated and used up. It was all so real to her.

Boundless creative fulfillment was only one of the by-products of Genevieve's amazing endeavors. What she was also doing was exploring new levels about people and their interactions. Her movies and her scripts indicated her uncanny ability to question and often understand, with startling boldness and clarity, human nature. I found it fascinating to watch and to ponder. It was so clear that much of the appeal came back to the fact that when she worked through her dolls, she could control the "socialness" of the event. In other words, she interacted with us *through* her dolls, rather than with us directly. And because it was controlled through her scripts, she could present her perceptions and observations of what she saw in the world around her, on her own terms. Through her movies, she gained enormous confidence in her own abilities and in the comfort level she felt amongst us, her family.

Somewhere along the way came the invasion of the Spice Girls. They invaded everyone's radio at that time, and they invaded us, the loyal members of Genevieve's audience. Her thirty minute but very insightful Barbie doll movies made way for less-enticing Spice Girl concerts. Armed with her collection of twenty-five Spice Girl dolls, each elaborately dressed, she presented cute but very long and drawn-out concerts in the glittery concert hall that Sydney and I had painstakingly designed and built for her. Some of these concerts lasted for twenty-one songs. Every couple of weeks, she'd make and sell tickets and we'd be gasping, thinking: "Oh another Saturday night concert in the basement!"

Hayden was absolutely spellbound by her concerts; Kobe was compassionate and did his best to not loose his grip completely. Sydney was more proactive with her "if you can't beat 'em, join 'em" approach and focused on adding Christmas lights for special effects or insisting that we dress up and make a night of it. The most memorable was the night the guys dressed up in suits and ties, and the girls in high heels, evening dresses and feather boas. That was the fun part of the night (don't forget: we didn't get out much!). Genevieve of course, was thrilled.

But the reality was, Genevieve was twelve. By now, her peers had long since put away their Barbie and Spice Girl dolls. Hmmm; how do I put those words down in black and white for you to read without feeling that I have just insulted her? Yes, it was true that her peers had grown beyond dolls but then they didn't *need* dolls the way Genevieve did. And it wasn't so much that she was playing *with* them, she was *exploring* and *researching* with them and she was gaining insight on levels that was miles beyond her peers! And she had the determination to overcome obstacles in her life that her peers couldn't even have imagined.

Genevieve's life was very much a fascinating mixture of her need and passion for creativity, contrasted by her need for order. She would eat up award shows, the *Guinness World Book of Records* and books on trivia. She loved "TV Guide Tuesdays" because she could put her feet up and sift through the TV week, even though she actually watched very few shows. When she was eleven, she astounded us when she listened to the "Top 95 Songs" of the year on New Year's Eve, carefully writing all ninety-five hits in order. The next day, we could ask her any number and she could answer with the corresponding song; likewise, we could give her the name of a song and she could tell us its number on the countdown. Many she could even tell us from the previous year's countdown. It was unbelievable.

At home, Genevieve almost always insisted on eating on her own and still struggled to hold conversations, much less initiate them. She had such genuine effervescence and would flit in and out of our lives in the course of each day, sprinkling her wonderful bits of humor and pink sparkle, then retreat back to the safety of her bedroom. She loved to slip into her pajamas and literally lock herself in her room (each child had a lock on their door because of Hayden's rampages). There she would recharge, through writing, drawing and music; and her skills were diversifying rapidly.

Often, I or sometimes Nolan would venture into her room to visit briefly. Sometimes she seemed genuinely glad to have us and would snuggle up warmly; but when she had had enough of us, which was usually after only a few minutes, her body language told us she was equally happy to get back to whatever she was doing. On Saturday nights, she would occasionally invite a friend for a sleepover, or entertain us with one of her self-directed movies or concerts; but her favorite activity was her "Saturday night one-person parties". She would crank up the tunes, draw, write, dance around and make no apologies for enjoying her time on her own. In fact, like most other things, she approached her parties with a sense of humor. Frequently, earlier on in the day, she would invite one of us to join her that evening and then giggle and say: "Oops, sorry! It's a one-person party and that means just me!"

One memorable afternoon, when Genevieve's limited interactions sent a familiar wave of "neglectful mom guilt" over me, I pretty much invited myself into her room and we just "hung out". To my surprise, later that same evening she said very sweetly and innocently: "This afternoon when you were here and then you left, I felt something I don't usually feel: I felt lonely". I was taken aback.

Chapter 26

As oddly insightful as Genevieve was, much of the time her emotions were like a mess of tangled wires. That was in part, why she often over-reacted and lashed out. I was desperate to find a way to smooth her emotions out, to lay them in front of her, and to teach her to label and understand each one. I knew she possessed the ability to understand them; the trick was to untangle the mess that was so frequently misfiring in her head and in her body. From that challenge and that desire, came one of our most successful and important strategies. It was a true conglomeration of Dr. Bryson's insight and experience combined with my specific knowledge of Genevieve, her life experiences and how her mind and body worked.

Dr. Bryson's concept was for Genevieve and me to write in a journal together each night, about the day's events. At the end of each entry, I was to draw a circle. As she and I re-capped the day, I would ask her to draw pie-slice shapes within the circle to represent in size the magnitude of the various feelings she had experienced during the course of the day. He referred to it as a "Feeling Wheel". But prior to embarking on this journal, I took the concept one step further, motivated by the deep feelings of *color* that I personally had always felt whenever thoughts of Genevieve entered my mind.

I chose "color" because there was just simply something about her effervescence that presented itself to me in terms of colors. I knew it was triggered specifically *by* her because it wasn't how I saw or experienced my other three children. Even when she was very little, whenever I closed my eyes and let myself feel Genevieve and feel her world, it always came boldly and beautifully to me in colors, most of them swirling. It was a world of colors, of pinks and of fluffiness. Even the colors I felt when she was angry or threatened and lashing out at the world, had that abstract, flowing and fluffy quality to them. In creating this strategy, I thought back to what I had read about colors and their impact in Donna Williams' book, and I think Dr. Bryson had mentioned something about colors as well. I can't really remember; I just remember the overwhelming feeling that through colors, Genevieve would best be able to pull out the emotions that were inside her, and safely lay them out and look at them.

I remember sitting down with her on the living room couch, a wide array of paint chips between us. She and I talked about feelings, emotions and colors, letting each one of them permeate through her and within her. We were both spellbound! I think for her, it was because she could then reach down to our stack of paint chips and match the color that she was feeling and experiencing. I was spellbound because I had the privilege of watching this wonderful and exciting process!

That afternoon, the process just got better and more exciting as I then let Genevieve's true self put her own words to her colors. Some were more graphic than others. She had different levels for emotions; the positive ones ranged from "happy" to "jubilant"; and for the more negative ones, she chose words like "threatened, impulsive, gloomy, angry" and the most intense and raw being: "got my shot gun mad". They certainly represented the vibrant person that she was.

She and I were so deeply connected that Saturday afternoon. The next step was to find pencil crayons that matched the array of emotions Genevieve had chosen. With tiny little labels I wrote on each pencil crayon, the emotion it depicted. The final step was to create a board, with a chart that had a swatch of each color, with the matching emotion listed below it. This chart, along with her carefully-labeled pencil crayons, she would keep with her journal, for us to refer to each night when we wrote together and filled out the Feeling Wheel.

The success of the Feeling Wheel/Journal was groundbreaking. I can't stress enough how important this process and strategy were. Much of the success was in the "marketing": it had to look enticing to Genevieve but not silly, pretentious and certainly not patronizing. Each night in the haven of Genevieve's bedroom, she and I could sort through and smooth out the tangled web of emotions of that day. The key was that she wasn't sorting them so much by the label and the term she used to describe them. It's important to understand that and make that distinction to see *why* this concept worked. She sorted them by the *color* that she *felt* when she relived the experience of them. Through colors she felt safe and they came from within her, sometimes bursting forth. That's what was so important: they came *from* her, as opposed to me or Genevieve herself, trying to pull them out. Together, we could then physically and visually acknowledge them, and release them as she drew them onto the pie-shaped wedges of her Feeling Wheel. By then studying the colors that she had drawn and the size of wedge that they filled, we could measure how much of an impact they had made in her day.

What was equally important was that I was now being kept abreast of issues going on in Genevieve's life, particularly school issues, which I was not present to witness. This was another ground-breaking result of the Feeling Wheel/Journal. Like so many children with autism, Genevieve could be seriously impacted upon by events earlier in the day, but then "shelve them" the moment she got home, as if they hadn't even happened. The problem was, at some point, they would come out or even worse, they would smolder away unrecognized. That had been the case of all the events that had lead to her grade five breakdown. Throughout her life there were times when I could see signs in her and carefully probe for information about what I thought might be bothering her; but often she would shut down and block it. It would then remain trapped, like a lurking creature hidden deep inside a closet, inevitably waiting to jump out. At the very least that "creature" would taint the sense of serenity that she would have otherwise felt, had it been recognized and addressed.

Often "shelving experiences" was a natural autism survival instinct that on some level, she was probably quite aware of doing. But often she wasn't even aware of their presence within her. That was because of the way she experienced things and how she processed those experiences: it was like they came into her system on an extraordinarily physical level, but she didn't have the tools to actually acknowledge them, much less deal with them. The result would be that they would get compartmentalized without her even being aware of them. With the Feeling Wheel/Journal, we had a vehicle to uncover many of the hidden stresses and to creatively address them.

The beauty of our process wasn't limited to exploring "traumas", whether they were little ones or deeply concerning ones. It was also a fabulous way of exploring and celebrating the good ones. It's important to remember that for a child with autism, an influx of positive and exciting experiences and emotions can be just as overwhelming as negative ones. As Dr. Bryson had described, the Feeling Wheel/Journal was a way of pictorially showing her that in a given day, she could experience a vast array of emotions, or in her terms, colors; yet at the end of the day, the "pie" was complete, a round shape and that overall, it had been a good day.

Very quickly, Genevieve lapped up our concept and she and I worked on it consistently for two years. It was a very precious and meaningful time for both of us and no matter how stressful or hectic my schedule had been, our evening Feeling Wheel/Journal time was always a favorite part of my day. Often it was hard and very draining work, especially if we uncovered an issue that was complex; but it was always fascinating and it meant the world to me because I could get inside her head and her life on a very deep level. It had been a long time coming.

Genevieve became very skilled at connecting with her feelings, and of smoothing them out, labeling them, and sorting them when they were a "tangled mess". The concept and the process moved mountains! To this day, there are still times when she struggles and stumbles with the onslaught of emotions; but it's nothing like before. Occasionally she and I still journal together when we need to and though the actual Feeling Wheel is tucked away in the past, and we have gloriously moved beyond it, there are times when she and I dust off her labeled pencil crayons and explore away!

Chapter 27

As a family, we kept it hidden from Genevieve, but we didn't share her devastation when Geri Haliwell left the Spice Girls, which soon lead to the group's break-up. We'd had enough of them on the radio and in our basement on Saturday nights. At least Genevieve's Barbie doll movies had intricate and interesting plots but the Spice Girl concerts were tough to handle. There was no character development and to be honest, how much of their music could you listen to? She was devastated by the break-up but like the true survivor that she was, she instinctively sought out a new passion; and she latched onto it like love at first sight: the reality show *Survivor*.

Genevieve took to the *Survivor* series like nothing else. It was so fitting, because in the real game of life, she was one of the ultimate survivors! To those of us who really know Genevieve, we all see her name as being synonymous with *Survivor*. Dating back to when she was very little, she was forging ways to enable herself to survive; it was a conscious effort on her part to survive and to beat the odds. She saw herself as a survivor and within that context it was no surprise that she would have felt such a deep connection and interest in the show and all of its characters.

Her new passion lead to awesome explorations and a new means for her to pursue the ever-intriguing world of people, their personalities, their character flaws and everything in between. And unlike her dolls, animal figurines and her scripts, these were real people and she was captivated. Season after season, she poured herself into the world of *Survivor*, often obsessing about it but always learning from it. Now, instead of Barbie movies and Spice Girls concerts, she presented us with intricate "Survivor" stories that she created. She read them to us, one episode at a time, complete with detailed, hand-drawn characters and ballots for us to vote at our own "tribal council". She had the official soundtrack and skillfully (after carefully rehearsing it in the privacy of her room), played segments in the background to perfectly match our actions as we cast our votes, which were then read by her.

Once again, as a family we were very much torn between our fascination for Genevieve's skill, her talent in her craft and the fact that she was letting us in; that told us we were important to her. But she expected and demanded far too much from us. Her scripts were wonderful but there were so many characters for us to familiarize ourselves with. Often a few weeks would pass in between readings of her episodes and yet she would expect us to have remembered the tiniest of details. It was tough enough for Nolan and me; but for Sydney and Kobe, who were then thirteen and fifteen, it was becoming more than a chore. Hayden had become such a destructive and complicated force that he couldn't join us and keeping him away during her readings added a new level of anxiety for each of us.

Luckily, Genevieve's passion and appetite for *Survivor* also inspired her to write her own school Survivor series, using her actual grade seven classmates as characters! Her ability to capture through her episodes, their personalities, their strengths and their weaknesses, and to reveal what she considered their flaws and true nature, was simply phenomenal. She certainly proved her ability to write with wit and sarcasm. Her "immunity challenges" were intriguing but what were even more intriguing were the interactions between her characters.

Genevieve's portrayals were bitingly accurate. One classmate was represented as a character who chose to take for her "luxury item", a push-up bra. (I have to say, when I saw this girl a couple of years later, I was impressed by Genevieve's foresight). Her class was mesmerized and in response, the teacher gave her class time to read each episode aloud. In fact, that was how Mrs. Jackson often bribed the class to complete their work on time: their reward would be permission to gather around Genevieve, listen to another episode and fall into the webs that she could weave! Several times I saw them, outside on a sunny day, with Genevieve in the middle, basking in her literary glory, the class encircling her and listening to her every word. They loved the antics of "their" character and they would marvel at her uncanny ability to pick up on the character subtleties of her peers and expand on them through her writing. I think they were equally impressed that she had the courage to be so bold. It was worrisome how some might respond, seeing themselves depicted so honestly. But I think they could see that she was accurate, she was honest and she was genuinely talented.

The "Grade Seven Survivor Series" was one of the many literary creations that lead Genevieve's teacher to make the comment to me, that there was "no way a typical grade seven could write like that!" It really was an amazing irony that someone who had had to be taught emotions, and basically how to respond, could now write so insightfully, about people, personalities and emotions.

For the Amity School Talent Show, it wasn't that Genevieve jumped at the chance to perform; it was more like she was driven. With no dance training, she cleverly choreographed a routine to Gloria Gaynor's song "I Will Survive". Shortly into the routine, she strategically slipped off an over-sized coat to reveal the *Survivor* logo that she and I had meticulously recreated. She danced with one other prop: a torch (unlit). It was her replica of the torches used at each tribal council and it was deeply representative of her own personal, lifelong quest: a quest to survive! She danced from her heart and her unique soul, and was rewarded with great applause and high acclaim.

Genevieve shone, being put on a pedestal and being appreciated and acknowledged for her unique talent. But her remarkable social insight continued to be stonewalled by her difficulty in carrying it over to her personal life. The girls in her age group were again becoming more rigid in their need to conform as a group and were less accepting of girls like

Genevieve who didn't fall into their molds. It was heart-wrenching, after years of cultivating relationships. Much of the purpose, afterall, of our many, brilliantly-themed parties and of my Children's Theatre group had been very strategic. But there was only so much that we could control and maintain when we were fighting the power of peer pressure and pre-teens spreading their wings and trying to find their way in the world. It wasn't so much a case of any of them being malicious or purposefully hurtful as it had been back in grade five. It was more that they were on completely different wavelengths.

Often, Genevieve felt left out and frequently referred to herself as "the invisible girl". In truth, often she was left out but more times, she was included. But it was her increasing social discomfort that didn't allow her to see it. She wasn't able to keep up with conversations and her headspace was so very different from the others. She turned inward and instead of talking to them, she talked out loud to herself, bringing negative attention and further widening the gap.

Chapter 28

Our home offered a joyful refuge from the often stressful and empty times Genevieve experienced in the world outside our walls. But within our walls, loomed and brooded the presence of Hayden. His battles with the outside world raged on and took its toll on each of us. Genevieve's life was profoundly affected by him, to the degree that even when he was calm and trying to be brotherly towards her, the scars were too deep and the memories and connections she made with him were too far reaching. It was controllable in the sense that she could stay clear of him much of the time, by remaining in her room where she longed to be anyway. But it was terribly draining for me because I was caught in the middle, constantly pulled in opposite directions. They both depended on me enormously; yet I could not safely have both of them in the same room together, much less do an activity with both. And I knew, or could only imagine, how much energy poor Genevieve wasted dealing with warding off Hayden and the parts of her mind and body that were filled with past experiences of him.

Propelled by an intense desire to improve the situation between Genevieve and Hayden, a path was forged and a real miracle fluttered into our lives: an incredible art therapist named Madeleine. Someone, I don't even remember who, suggested trying art therapy with Genevieve. At that point we really didn't know anything about it, but we were so desperate to make changes that when I sought out funding from a local organization, I think there was desperation in my voice that resonated and made them want to choose us as the family that they would provide funding for. I was moved beyond tears because it was virtually the first time in Genevieve's life, that her needs had taken precedence over Hayden's. Until then, his extreme behaviors had overshadowed the bulk of behavioral therapist's time and she received what morsels were left over. This was just for her and it was a form of therapy that had her name written all over it!

For Madeleine's orientation, it was a labor of love for me to dig through boxes and binders to compile a spectrum of Genevieve's creations throughout the years. I laid out, chronologically, samples from when she could very first deal with holding a pencil until the current time. Each gave an amazing glimpse into her emotional stage of development at the time it was created, and her ability and desire to reach out to people *through* her characters. Exemplified through her art and her writing was that concept of having a "middleman" to buffer the "socialness" and hold the world safely at arm's length. The simple, basic drawings of the early years quickly progressed into the longer and more complex creations of the day, such as her fascinating and insightful versions of teen magazines, hilarious parodies of *Survivor* and her clever, comical mockeries of everyday life.

As fate would have it, it turned out that Madeleine's focus could not be predominantly on Hayden, as we had planned. He was too formidable an issue in Genevieve's life, one that had to be handled extremely carefully or she would simply shut down. The most she was willing to do was to occasionally bring him into their drawings, which she did by depicting him as a tiny bug under her shoe, which she then squished. Oh Genevieve!

It was frustrating because throughout her life, Genevieve could talk very openly with me about her frustrations, fear, and distaste for her brother. I was grateful for that, because she needed that outlet and I was carefully able to chip away at removing the guilt that she sometimes felt for not feeling more warmth towards him. But the bottom line was also the fact that I was *his* mom too, and it was a complex, heart-wrenching position to be put in. She needed someone other than me to confide in and to access parts of her heart, her mind and her body that could allow her to heal. That was part of Madeleine's role.

Madeleine was remarkably intuitive and perceptive in following Genevieve's lead with respect to Hayden, and she was patient, ever chipping away in tiny, calculated steps. Still, as deeply connected to Madeleine as Genevieve was, it would take years before she could actually bring Hayden's name into their conversations and speak with any level of candor. But in addition to the issue of Hayden, the mound of issues that surfaced in Genevieve's life during her high school years was more than enough to fill Madeleine's time and energy.

The incredible work and the deep, reciprocal relationship that Madeleine and Genevieve have carefully crafted together has been a miracle. And their relationship has been mutually beneficial. I know that Madeleine herself would step in at this point and be very forthright in describing the depths of insight and inspiration that she has personally gained from her years in accompanying our heroine on her journey. That simply is who Genevieve is!

My heart is very much "aflutter" as I write these paragraphs because of the role that Madeleine has played in Genevieve's life and the support she has given me. She came into our lives like a tiny hummingbird, fluttering with energy and emotion. She has the brightest eyes and an insatiable appetite for "chipping away", for finding ways to heal and explore. Despite her talent, there were times when she pushed a little too hard and Genevieve pushed her away; it still happens sometimes, as it does to me. But Madeleine consistently finds ways to skillfully and lovingly get back in.

Madeleine became Genevieve's confidante and mine. Next to me, she is the person who knows Genevieve best. And despite the close bond that Genevieve and I have always shared, she and I are, afterall, "mom and daughter" and it would have been unrealistic back then, as it would be now, to think that Genevieve would keep me privy to all of her thoughts and experiences. By the age of twelve, she was a passionate, gifted writer and artist who created from her heart and from her body, with little holding back; much of her creations were filled with intense emotion and descriptions and not necessarily things she felt appropriate for her mom to read. I respected her right to privacy when she pushed away repeated reminders that my degree in English Literature allowed me to experience a piece of literature, simply on its own merit, without necessarily connecting it to its author. It was disappointing that she kept so many of her creations secret; but I was all the more grateful that she had someone like Madeleine with whom she could trust and look to for advice, with not only the content of what she was writing but the technical side as well.

It's so important to reinforce to parents, that a therapist for a child as complex as one with autism, is not simply someone you keep in the wings to jump in and assist you when there is a crisis. When things are running smoothly, that is *not* the time to pull back and put the therapist on the back burner. The calm times are when they both work just as hard together, in addressing the day-to-day challenges: call it personal development. It's pretty hard to accomplish those goals if your therapist is only around when you are in crisis!

It would take pages and pages to describe what a godsend it has been to me personally, to have someone close to Genevieve, who has become so skilled in the "language of Genevieve". Madeleine has not only been an accomplice for me to strategize with for the tough issues, but also a partner to celebrate the amazing and successful ones with. At times I have felt a little envious of the things that Genevieve will share with Madeleine, but all I have to do is look at the big picture and remind myself that between what Genevieve offers up to me and what she presents to Madeleine, we have a very clear picture of who she is and how we can best assist her. I add to that, the phenomenal insight and support that Dr. Bryson offers, and there is a picture of a young woman who is very much a work in progress but very well supported, understood and appreciated.

The importance of Madeleine's role is heightened by her dedication to Genevieve and to our family. There have been times, some of them months at a stretch, when I have succumbed to stress and depression, and had to say to Madeleine: "Can you be there for Genevieve because I have to let myself crash, so that I can climb back up again and be strong?" Each time, she stepped in and offered to Genevieve, and to me, her unspoken support. I wouldn't have been able to do that without her. She has been more than a gift. She has truly been one of our miracles!

Chapter 29

The transition to High School was huge and I was mortified. Genevieve was entering a world where teachers didn't know her, and where the student population was triple that of Amity Elementary. There were bigger halls and bigger expectations, both academically and socially and the gap was growing. This wasn't a world where we could, as a family, guide her socially and emotionally, by using parties and theatrical performances. The countless scenarios that she had captured in her scripts and "movies" were now the real thing: teenage angst and drama. She'd had a taste of it in elementary school and had barely survived it; how would she manage in this environment where it could be even more confusing and suffocating?

That summer, those weeks before the new school year began, I felt something I'd never felt before: *fear*. It was real fear, the kind where I would wake up at 5:00am with shooting pains in my stomach, or crying in my sleep. Until that point, I had always had faith that if we just educated the people around Genevieve and enabled them to embrace her amazing spirit, accept her challenges and uniqueness, then success would follow. But this was a different world. Though she had more determination and courage than anyone I knew, could she handle the challenges in leaving the childhood and well-supported Amity world behind?

I knew in my heart the answer lay, where it has always laid, in welcoming and enticing the world around her, to be a part of her world. That was how she would adapt and grow, and how they would, in turn, learn from her. For me, the best place was to pick up a pen. It all started with a single word: effervescence. It was the word that best described Genevieve and who she was, a beautiful, wild angel whose feet never quite touched the ground.

One single, little word and all I had to do was close my eyes, think and feel Genevieve and from that emerged the first little tale, from which this book would eventually arise. It was much shorter, as many important events of our heroine's life were slashed to keep it at a length that would intrigue but not overwhelm the high school staff. They, the staff of Parkplace Secondary, were receptive and I do believe that the one hundred hours that went into the creation of "Effervescence" helped to open their eyes and hearts, allowing them to very quickly have insight into Genevieve and the challenges that lay ahead.

It was intriguing how Genevieve responded to the concept of a "book" being written about her, even if it was intended for distribution simply amongst school staff, family and support agencies. I couldn't, in fairness to her, create it without her knowledge. I asked for her permission, hoping that she would see it as another form of our team approach. What I didn't anticipate was the keen interest she took in reading it when it was completed.

I was to be honest, a little apprehensive that her self esteem might take a few blows from some of the candid descriptions of her past and current challenges and behaviors. If that was the case, her self esteem was seemingly boosted by the more prevalent descriptions of her extraordinary abilities and her genuine uniqueness. It reminded me of the time, way back in elementary school when I found her perusing the Home/School communication book that her teachers and I shared to keep each of us up-to-date with her progress. That day I was horrified because many of our remarks were open and revealing accounts of day to day issues. To my utter surprise, she smiled back smugly and said: "I just like to snoop through my own life sometimes...but boy, you really dig deep in to my soul!" She didn't seem at all perturbed or invaded; it was quite the opposite. I saw a look of mature gratitude, because she knew we were all working together as a team to "cheer her along" and to find answers to the tough issues that she faced.

I think Genevieve was quite mesmerized and proud of the shining and very colorful character that she saw portrayed in those communication books, as she was with the same heroine portrayed in "Effervescence". Interestingly, I discovered that she also loved to read through her Feeling Wheel/Journal, like she was reading the chapters of a really good book. It was amazing to witness and to interpret because it was like she could take herself off a shelf, examine herself, learn from the experience and then put herself back up on the shelf, where it could gather some dust until the next time she felt the need or the desire to learn a little bit more. I am certain that every time she pulled herself off of that shelf, her hungry and clever eyes found something new, something a little deeper than the time before. It was utterly fascinating! She was utterly fascinating!

High school did offer features that we hadn't anticipated. Genevieve immediately responded to the more mature relationship between teachers and students; and the lockers provided an important sense of security and individuality because hers could be her tiny refuge, decorated with her unique artistic flair. Though she no longer had a special education assistant within her classroom, she did have access to a Learning Assistance room where she could seek out help and have time to herself to tune out and recharge.

The biggest bonus of high school was a well-established drama department. That was Genevieve's place to shine and to be herself. It was what saved her. In her drama classes and in her roles in their school plays and performances, she could step in and out of character roles for the sheer fun of it, and to survive. And what Genevieve did have, was courage! In her new environment her bravery and determination were remarkable and inspirational. Often she existed as she had always done, alongside of her peers; sometimes she interacted naturally and sometimes she sought out solitude.

As Genevieve's team, we all felt that a "Leaving School" certificate, as opposed to the traditional "Dogwood" was the most attainable goal. That goal in itself would necessitate, as in elementary school, team work to mold an academic and arts based program that she could realistically handle. She trudged along, juggling her talent in English, Drama and Art with her struggles in Math and Sciences, some of them gradually modified to ensure a reasonable degree of success.

Despite her determination, the social component of Parkplace complicated the delicate balance that made up each day. Genevieve's masking skills developed even more precariously and the face she presented to staff and students was, once again, not an accurate description of what was going on. Many times she broke down into tears, drawing negative attention to herself. She was once again, falling apart at the seams. It became another complex and emotionally-charged predicament. In some respects, her tears sometimes instilled an element of empathy and compassion amongst peers who acted kindly and supportively towards her. But in the safety of her home, she referred to herself at school as "Elizabeth thrown into the Samburu tribe". In *Survivor* terms, it meant, the gentle sweetheart of the good tribe being thrust into the depths of a ferocious and foreign tribe. More modifications were made and they helped; but it was the drama department that got her through. The long-awaited art classes that she'd had such high hopes for back in elementary school were such a disappointment to her and caused great anxiety and disconnection. As good as the art teacher was, Genevieve created from such a place of rawness and unique perspective that she found these classes stifling, rigid and conventional. They didn't offer her a creative outlet; they made her want to crawl out of her skin.

At times during the early years of high school, Genevieve expressed feelings of depression; but there were always enough glimmering moments, combined with that precious recovery time at home, which kept her state of mind from really being seen for what it was: *in* a state of depression.

Genevieve was driven to accomplish the goals she set in her own mind and to appear to be as "typical" as she could. She knew that high school was a necessary evil and did her best to reap what positive she could from it. Her three years at Parkplace could be described as tolerable, though it was not to say she didn't enjoy her time there. She did have many wonderful experiences and was liked and respected by all of the staff and many of her peers; but a part of her did repress and shut down. We could see it in her but it was gradual and we questioned that maybe it was just part of growing up. It was her "effervescence"; it just wasn't pink and glowing and pillowy soft anymore. It really wasn't until she left Parkplace and moved to an even bigger and more overwhelming senior high school that she herself, would see how much she had recoiled, and how much she had in fact, been suffering from depression.

Chapter 30

Throughout high school, much of Genevieve's life still teetered on the contradiction of her desire to let the world in versus the need and desire to keep it out. She loved and cherished her solitary time yet yearned to have a greater connection with friends. "Her world", her escape from reality as she called it, was so very much made up of "soft and fluffy pink clouds" and could be a delightful place to be. But that fluffy pinkness also acted as a barrier between her and the outside world, whether it was with her family or the more distant world at large. At times, she felt heart-wrenching loneliness.

The evening of Sydney's eighteenth birthday, when Genevieve was barely fifteen, stands out in my mind as one of the most memorable and monumental experiences that I've had with her. It was a very personal moment that I hesitate to share with the world; but as I remember only a few specific details, only the sheer intensity of the experience, I think it is okay for me to pass it on to you. Very simply, Genevieve let me in to a place in her heart and her head and her spirit, on a level that had me literally shaking with wonder, for three days after.

It was a simple conversation, a very tearful one on her part. We were up in her safe-haven bedroom, as we listened to Sydney and her friends partying in the rooms below. As fate would have it, it happened on an evening when I was completely drained after

Nolan and I had just returned from what had turned out to be one our most harrowing experiences in a mall with Hayden. I think the presence of Sydney's friends in our home, the happy sounds and the music, triggered feelings in Genevieve on a level she had never been able to access before. I can't even remember her exact words or her thoughts because it was so intense and I was so drained; but it was about loneliness, about autism and about being trapped. She cried and cried and there was something in the way that she hugged me and the way that she genuinely wanted to hug me, that was like nothing I had ever felt from her before. It was indescribable, like literally a magnetic force, but more than that. There was a look in her eye, a level of trust and of getting through a locked door that no one else had been able to pass, because she hadn't until then, been prepared to let them.

But she let me in and I did literally shake for three days afterwards, as I am shaking now as I retell it. The next morning, I had to teach my dance class, which I could barely do. I had to flat out tell my students that I had had the most amazing experience with my autistic child and that I would do my best to stay focused, but that I made no promises! They looked back at me with a mixture of wonder, excitement and not really being able to know what the hell I was talking about.

Chapter 31

How do you help someone to feel more comfortable and able to converse naturally with the people around them, when they have a disorder that prohibits it, one that doesn't offer them the necessary "hardware" to make it just "happen?" That was Genevieve's greatest challenge; it still is. I was desperate to find ways to cross that bridge, to make it happen; but how? So many of us had worked on it for years; *she* had worked on it for years. How do you combat loneliness and the desire to connect with people, without that natural ability? How do you do it with the additional challenge of a body and a sensory system that responds so *dramatically* and so *physically?*

Those were daunting questions. Throughout Genevieve's life, we had proven time and time again that her conversational skills were very closely linked to her feeling accepted and at peace with herself and the environment around her. In scrutinizing those questions my mind raced, but with a sinking heart, to a Saturday afternoon a couple of years prior. Genevieve and I had had a rare opportunity to have the house to ourselves and she was very relaxed and at peace. When my niece Bella arrived, to arrange a baby shower for her sister, I was shocked to see Genevieve leave the security of her bedroom to join us. She was very animated and excited to have Bella there and she plopped herself down on the couch with her legs outstretched across mine, a sign that she was eager to connect with us but needed support.

As Bella and I talked, I gently massaged Genevieve's feet, knowing it helped to keep her relaxed and grounded. But it was a harsh eye opener to see that even in that calm and very controlled setting, she struggled to converse. Bella had very close ties to our family and had, in fact lived with us for one week each month, for several years, when her dad was out of town. Genevieve and Bella had mutual adoration and respect for each other; yet still, that afternoon Genevieve struggled. She blurted out random thoughts, some of them literally mid sentence. At times, she came right out and said: "I don't know what to say". Finally, out of confusion, frustration and discomfort, she flitted away and headed back to her room. Bella and I were left looking at each other, our hearts feeling more than a little broken.

That incident and many more, ran through my mind the night of Sydney's birthday party. Genevieve's heart-wrenching revelation brought home the need to conquer this challenge about conversing and socializing. The stakes were high and given her history of countless examples like the one with my niece Bella, I was feeling less than optimistic. To relate this issue in the terms of how I saw Genevieve's world being made of colors, with her happy and relaxed state being one of pink and fluffiness and of clouds, "conversing" was the one area where all I could see and feel in her was simply white clouds. They were clouds with no depth or fluffiness to them. It was like that white mass that sometimes fills the sky, more like a thick blanket. *How could we put color and texture into them?* We'd tried for so long in so many ways. It was nebulous, not a skill that could easily be taught. It had to come from within her and that was where she was most trapped.

I won't say I gave up hope, but it felt insurmountable. Was this ultimately a hurdle that even Genevieve and all her determination and creativity couldn't jump over? And how would the looming onset of senior high school factor into all of this? It seemed insurmountable.

Chapter 32

*O*ddly enough, advancement to senior high school showed us what had been missing in Genevieve and what had been slowly stomped out during the three junior high years that had preceded it: it was her effervescence! As her family, we hadn't really been able to put our finger on it because it did happen in increments, a slow suppressing process; but it had faded.

Ironically, Clairefield Senior was an even bigger school than Parkplace, triple in size, making it six times the size of her original school environment at Amity. Yet in this environment Genevieve could dare to be more herself, to let her unique effervescence shine. She had a knack for putting together off-beat outfits, that were just a little bit quirky, with interesting accessories that made her feel unique and "in character" enough to feel safe. Some were outlandish like neon scrunchies made of fake hair, or a top hat. But she had a way of pulling it off because she had such a lack of ego. She dressed from her heart and her very creative and beautiful spirit. She dressed for herself and for no one else.

With a student population of about twelve hundred, the price she paid with the increase of social presence and chaos was made up for by the fact that there were a greater number of peers who also dared to be a little bit quirky. She was accepted and most times blended in, not because she looked like everyone else, but because this was an environment where students were encouraged to be individuals. I think she must have been a little bit of a "walking museum" because her outfits were not outlandishly outspoken, but cleverly designed and accessorized.

In senior high, once again, Genevieve could float through the halls in her unique way, with her feet barely touching the ground. And the very best thing that this school could bring into her life was an extraordinary and well-established Drama and Musical Theatre department! Along with that came a group of kids who may not have been in her headspace, but they certainly shared a little piece of it. And the man who tied it all together was a truly phenomenal and gifted man who loved and celebrated every student he came in contact with. Genevieve was no exception and with his brilliance and his profound insight into human nature, it took him barely a glimpse to see the treasure that was Genevieve!

She had just over a year with him, before he was taken from the world by an illness; but in his subtle and often very far from subtle ways, he touched and altered her life deeply. *That* is actually an understatement. He *profoundly* touched and altered her life in far-reaching ways. There was absolutely no doubt that much of the resurgence of her effervescence was a result of his presence in her life!

It would be lying to say that the move to senior high was a new world that magically opened the door to two years of fun and success. True, there were glimmers of magic, especially the ones that exploded from within the theatre auditorium; but much was due to hard work, more soul searching and deeper explorations into "translating the world to Genevieve and translating Genevieve to the world". She worked hard and each of us, the growing members of her support team, worked as unobtrusively, yet still as creatively, as we could.

Grade twelve, Genevieve's graduating year, was what she would refer to as her "incomprehensible year", not only for challenges but for accomplishments! With the support and insight of Dr. Bryson and Madeleine, our strategies became even more complex but immensely fun and fascinating to create. Often the key to working with Genevieve, to help her to unravel and explore and decipher the mysteries around her, still lay within working through the concept of a "middle man" or a buffer. Sometimes I could simply draw (with my terribly inadequate drawing skills), sketches of our two miniature schnauzers. With their little pondering eyes, a simple tilt of their heads and bubble captions depicting them questioning what was going on, or by drawing them offering her suggestions, it was sometimes enough to allow Genevieve to look through different eyes, to either open up about an issue or to explore it.

Visualizations continued to be powerful in assisting her to gauge upcoming situations. By guiding her through visualizations, she could look at herself in the situation, to ponder and experience and actually see how it might feel. Then we could predict whether she could realistically handle them and if there were modifications that would be wise or necessary.

Vibrant, guided imagery type visualizations were one of my specialties and often proved to be a godsend in helping her to recover and relax from stressful or confusing situations. Many were born out of sheer desperation, in times when she did crash and needed to be picked up again. Often, I had to free up my head and do what had always worked best: to step back and *feel* Genevieve. It wasn't always easy, as that year seemed to be like an endless onslaught of "issue torpedoes", one after another, with little space in between. And they didn't always happen on art therapy days, when I could leave the issue to be addressed or unraveled by Madeleine and her creative insight and experience. Often, Genevieve would wait until late at night or just a few minutes before she was scheduled to leave for school, before dropping one on me.

Sometimes images came easily and all I had to do was feel Genevieve, feel zebra stripes, pink clouds and vibrant little images things that were safe and humorous to her; and then the story lines would just play in my mind that I could relay back to her. Sometimes, it was hard to find the energy to even let myself go there. But often I found that once I got myself over the hump of "Okay, I need an image and I need it now…" a little bit of magic happened and it became a delightful place for us both to be. Creating spontaneous images and storylines for her to drift off to sleep with were often for me, exhausting but always exhilarating. One of my favorites, on a particularly difficult night when I really didn't know if I had it in me to pull something unique and creative out, was an image of her on a beach with her current heart throb, him in a tux and her in a zebra-striped wedding dress. It was such fun for us both and it did the trick. It didn't necessarily solve the issue, but it did take the edge off of it.

As far as the exact nature of the work that she and Madeleine do together in their sessions, I only know bits and pieces of; but I've seen the sparkle in Madeleine's eyes and I know what is in Genevieve's, so I can hardly even imagine what creative sparks fly when the two of them submerge into Genevieve's haven!

Throughout senior high, the most complex challenge remained, as it always had been, that Genevieve wanted so desperately to fit in, yet knew herself well enough to be adamant that it couldn't be at the expense of loosing her identity. As bright and able as she was, she was still a person who was physically and mentally exhausted at the end of each school day. Simply being surrounded by hundreds of people, hour after hour was draining and she needed massive amounts of recovery time afterwards. Social time *had* to be offset by substantial time to herself, alone in her room, writing, drawing or working on the computer. She needed to recover. That was simply who she was; it was her reality and ours'. At home we accepted and respected that and built our lives around it.

During her "incomprehensible year", Genevieve learned what it was to fall in love and not have it returned or handled very well. That was tough, really tough. But ultimately, she learned volumes from it; and the young man involved learned about himself and his own serious shortcomings. In a gentle way, she came back stronger and experienced the realization that despite her challenges in understanding the emotional confusion of early adulthood, she had an insightful sense of "self" that this "typical" young man did not.

Genevieve also went to Cuba with her Musical Theatre group and had a fabulous time! It took planning, insight, support and recovery time; but she did it. She is simply the bravest and most determined person I have ever known.

Chapter 33

On answer to my earlier question of: "How do you teach someone with autism to converse naturally?" I'm sorry but I don't have magical answers. But I can offer some insight, because in the past couple of years, we have seen very measurable success. I am happy and not the least bit humbled to say that I was wrong, back when Genevieve was fifteen and I almost gave up hope, thinking she had come as far as she could come. *I was wrong*; I want to write that over and over and over. I don't know how much further she will get with these kinds of challenges, but I do know she's not done yet.

The answer to that question, at least for how it related to Genevieve was: you don't teach it. You do it by enabling her to feel safe and confident enough to let her guard down and feel accepted and respected. In her case, slowly it just happened: tiny little steps, bits of natural conversation that didn't happen before. It was and is a slow process; it has to be and with each new level of comfort, you, as team members, pray that the door will not close there. The best you can do is to keep those goals and those requirements at the forefront, and then you work hard but unobtrusively, and you pray. And then you take the time to stand back and celebrate and marvel at her courage and her spirit and at all of those little bits of magic! *There is magic in life, there truly is; but there is also something called hard work, and sticking to your guns and listening to your heart.* That is the path that Genevieve has chosen and that is the path that those of us who love and really know and understand her follow. We just keep a few steps ahead of her.

One of the pieces of "hard, yet unobtrusive work" came from a little catalyst, a team member who tumbled back into our lives. Tamantha, that was her name and I really think she was a little, perfectly-timed missing piece. It wasn't just her role; it was as much her personality. She was another of our blessings!

When I look at my family's journey, I can't help but smile and wonder: how many gains have been catapulted by a state of desperation, joined by a little timely stroke of luck? Even at some of our darkest moments many, many times things just fell together, all like a fusion of desperation, soul searching and timing. At this point, Genevieve's graduating year, I was feeling such intense sadness and frustration at seeing how seriously her conversational skills and lack of comfort were holding her back and damaging her self esteem. We had tried so many things over the years. The exercises presented by her behavioral therapist previously, had been far too juvenile and ineffective. Role playing was seen by her as obtrusive, phony and unnerving. It caused her to shut down in frustration and resentment, even though she knew and accepted it as a skill that she wanted to improve upon. I was desperate.

But like a force of nature, along came one of those surreal moments when things become so clear, the kind experience where you even remember exactly where you were standing, the season, even the time of day. I've had more than a few of those. In this case, I was walking our dogs with Hayden, deep in thought and desperately trying to come up with a plan. It just burst out at me and it filled my every thought: "We need to get Tamantha back!"

Tamantha was a life skills coach who had worked with Genevieve previously a couple of years prior, when we'd been given a one-year contract through a government agency. She had helped to broaden Genevieve's horizons a little and we had noticed a marginal improvement in her socializing skills. But there was now just something about where Genevieve was in her life and definitely something about Tamantha's unique personality and the relationship between them, that I was overtaken, knowing that *this* was the moment, that there was the potential to take things to a new level. Standing there on the sidewalk with Hayden and our two dogs, I knew it wasn't just that we needed someone in Tamantha's capacity; that wasn't it at all. We needed Tamantha!

The plan leapt out of me and had to be made a priority. When Hayden and I got back home with our dogs, I calculated and pondered and tried to come up with a financial plan because it would mean juggling our finances to pay for it ourselves. I felt sick because it wasn't a huge expense but our finances were so tight that it would impact us noticeably. And I hadn't heard from Tamantha for a long time; I didn't even know if she was still doing that kind of work, much less if she was available. There was a momentum going but could it all come together? I was scared to uncross my fingers or take a breath.

Literally, the very next morning, our phone rang. On the other end, as if by magic, was the coordinator for the same government agency; Genevieve's name had just come up on their waiting list. They were, once again, willing to pay for a life skills coach. Not only that, Tamantha was available and anxious to start back working with Genevieve! I could hardly believe our luck or the timing and I did not believe for even a moment that it was all simply a coincidence.

As a member of our team, Tamantha had specific goals and strategies that we had devised; but that wasn't the way she presented herself to Genevieve. She was a captivating, twenty-four year old with a solid background in Fine Arts and working with people with disabilities. She had natural beauty and elegance, inside and out, with just a little touch of quirkiness; and she was so genuine. She had an impressive ability to slide herself, along with her skills and her Fine Arts background, unobtrusively, into Genevieve's life. And, she had a natural flair for accessorizing with unique earrings and shoes! She and Genevieve made a perfect match.

Genevieve saw Tamantha as a mentor, a confidante and a friend. All of those things Tamantha was, and still is today. She deserves no end of accolade for her work and her subtle and strategic outings and activities, many of them related to Fine Arts. Through them, she was able to carefully target many issues without setting off Genevieve's radar. Through Tamantha's casual but careful modeling, Genevieve made huge strides in understanding how to present herself, and how to respond not only to clerks and attendants, but also to strangers and to friends. She learned skills and gained confidence in herself and who she was.

Tamantha was also able to offer insight from *her* vantage point, which was often different from what the rest of us saw. It was like finding little missing pieces to the puzzle of Genevieve. Madeleine and Dr. Bryson, for instance, generally saw her in controlled, comfortable environments. Tamantha could pinpoint strengths and weaknesses that she saw in the less predictable and less safe situations. Genevieve was so bright and so able on many levels of her life but there were huge gaps that needed to be acknowledged and addressed; many Nolan and I were well aware of but we needed someone of Tamantha's capacity to back us up. So, the addition of Tamantha's input, combined with the input from Madeleine, Dr. Bryson and myself gave us a very well-rounded picture of Genevieve.

Aside from Tamantha's personality and genuine talent, the "fairy dust" that made all the difference was the timing. Genevieve needed to branch out. There was only so much that she could learn from her family, or her therapists. She needed to be with someone "cool" that she trusted, who could take her, a little bit magically, into places so that she could enter them as the uniquely challenged but equally gifted teenage artist that she was. It *was* time!

To return once again to the question about conversing naturally: has there been success? Absolutely, and there will be more. There is no question about that. But it has to evolve, to be *allowed* to evolve in little ways and in little places, when it is meant to. Often we have been taken aback by the comfort level we see in Genevieve when she navigates through stores and restaurants, a naturalness that wasn't there before. We celebrate that but also live in the real world of remembering that there are still inconsistencies. Contributing factors can fall into play, at almost any given moment. Even with support, there are times when she becomes confused, overwhelmed and anxious. It is still not unheard of for her to have a meltdown using her bank card or having Christmas Dinner with relatives.

Genevieve is an intelligent, gifted young woman who remains uniquely effected by her environment, her sensory system, her emotions, and her difficulty in understanding the complex world around her. Potentially there are contributing factors, before, during and after *any* event or experience. That is just the reality. But if I were to create a picture, using images of fairies and heroines, to describe the backbone, the foundation and the underlying philosophy of what makes any of this work, two images rush to my mind. One would be that of an unscarred heart, one that feels accepted and at peace, a heart that is intricately connected to slowly-pulsating wings. The second would be the glorious glow of recovery time afterwards. Always, there *must* be recovery time, or there will be prices to pay.

Those two images, those components, are what work for the heroine of this tale. No matter what the inconsistencies or contributing factors in this heroine's life, those have remained absolutely consistent. That is what makes any success possible!

Chapter 34

At home, Genevieve continues to flit in and out of our lives. It's not that often that she will initiate conversation, even if she has something on her mind. Often there is silence, unless we are willing to start the conversation and work to keep it going. That's just who she is. For a long time I felt so much guilt if I didn't try to maintain the conversation, and often depleted myself doing so. One day, I finally just asked her. What I sensed from her response was threefold: some of the time, she feels awkward and that's probably why she flits off and leaves. Sometimes, she leaves because she got a little "fix" of us, had enough and wanted to go back to doing her own thing. To my surprise, many of the silences she is fine with; she doesn't necessarily want conversation returned, she simply wants to be in our presence.

Often when I'm home with Genevieve, I worry that she's lonely. Again, I finally asked her about it. Sometimes she does feel loneliness but much of the time, it's quite the opposite. I've learned that often it's simply my perception of what *I* would be feeling if I were in her shoes. But then I don't have autism. Much of her "alone times" she revels in and comes alive. And she isn't necessarily "alone". She is an artist, a writer and a creator. She is never completely alone. Sometimes she hovers around us, seemingly trying to connect. At times she can, and sometimes she struggles even making the attempt. I try to remind myself that if I'm not sure what it is that she wants, I should just ask. Much of the time, it works.

Reading Genevieve's body remains an art. As a family, we do instinctively word things carefully because she does experience interactions so physically. Because of the way her body is "wired", her point of reference is different, and so many things hold a different meaning for her or trigger reactions that would be different from us. She still has trouble seeing other people's point of view and can be rather scornful and unforgiving when she disagrees.

Eye contact, always one of the "hot" autism issues, remains an intriguing one. Genevieve did avoid it when she was young and often fought it; but now at the age of eighteen, it often does come quite naturally. I don't think it's just that she now understands that eye contact is an important part of communication; I think she genuinely feels the desire to make that connection. If she does feel the need to draw away, she does it more subtlety than in the past, at least when she's amongst people she is comfortable with. In a group setting or with people she's not connected to, she may tilt her head to the side and keep her eyes noticeably forward.

At times she unintentionally overuses eye contact, almost like she doesn't know when to turn it off. If she is expressing something emphatically to someone and she is intent on getting a response or an answer, she doesn't always recognize the subtlety of when to release her eyes. I find it can be a little bit unnerving, when I've released myself from her gaze and several seconds later, I find her still striving to meet my eyes; but I'm working on it.

Second only to writing and drawing, Genevieve's communication abounds most naturally through the computer. It is literally a lifeline. She has made and maintained many meaningful and important relationships, some of them for years. These friends see the true Genevieve because she can connect directly from her mind to theirs', without struggling with the awkward physical and social complications that would challenge her if they were physically in the same room with her.

On internet, she doesn't have to use up energy struggling with the turmoil of eye contact or feeling confused by her body language or theirs'. She connects with people who share common interests and who are just as passionate and knowledgeable as her. Japanese anime is one of her specialties and internet has been a fabulous resource for her to grow and develop artistically with, because many websites serve as a venue for writers and artists to post their work. Through this medium, she has, over the years, received much acclaim and recognition for her work from people that she values, people who are credible because they too are well-versed, gifted and inspired. Because she is so comfortable with this medium, and the people connected, she also values their criticisms and suggestions and learns from them.

Even back when Genevieve was in elementary school, when *Survivor* was at its peak, she was able to contribute to their website, her incredibly insightful and often bitingly satirical analyses of the different tribe members. We were in awe of the level of writing she was producing and the acknowledgement she received in praise of her work. Many of them led to great discussions amongst internet *Survivor* fans throughout the world. She was quite a motivator. She learned volumes about people, about personalities and about her own talent and her craft.

One of the internet features that means the world to Genevieve, is that her "colleagues and associates" see her and her work as coming purely from her, an artist, an illustrator and a writer, *not* an artist, an illustrator and writer who has autism. At this point in her life, that is imperative to her.

Some of Genevieve's computer time is just plain down time, like surfing to find snippets of favorite shows or perusing quirky accessories on-line. The list goes on and on. But it should not be seen as filler time. For someone like Genevieve, the typical stigma around computer time is invalid and should be re-evaluated. She does not use her computer to escape relationships in the outside world. She uses it to *enhance* them.

She learns and she grows. When she does use her computer to push away the world and recharge, it is because she has autism and she *needs* to have that time. If this were twenty years ago, before most homes had at least one computer, not many eyebrows would have been raised if she spent that same amount of time with a book in front of her. Think about it: producing artwork and writing, connecting with people who share your passions, interacting with them and learning from them... that is a lot more "social" than sitting behind a book.

For a time we did worry about internet predators, but experience has shown that when Genevieve is on the computer, she is not bombarded by outside and social stimuli and her senses are probably *more* acute than the average teen. Ironically, just a few days before writing these paragraphs, Genevieve had an article published in our local newspaper. In her article, she expressed her intense resentment towards people who assume that all teens enter chat rooms, abuse their computers and put themselves at risk. Her article was well written and genuine. She gave helpful tips to children and teens about how they could protect themselves from questionable people and how to detect and deal with them should problems arise. Some of it comes back to "autism rule-based behavior": she has an extremely strong sense of right and wrong, which she does not cross and she openly scorns those who do.

As has been the case with many of Genevieve's precious things, there have, at times, been complex strings attached to the computer. But always the "little strings" of her life have held open or pulled open little doors that have helped to solve the mysteries of Genevieve and of autism. There was one involving our computer that was very stressful and intense, especially for her; but it was fascinating. It opened up a new door for Genevieve, for us and now for you, in understanding how intricately the mind, the body and experiences, are all linked for someone with autism. It unfolds in the remaining paragraphs of this chapter.

A year ago, quite out of the blue, Genevieve was literally writhing in pain for hours, screaming about a severe toothache. Her teeth were absolutely flawless so it made no sense. As she lay in tears with her head in my lap, she and I carefully dissected all of the events and sensations of the day, and the days that preceded it. The pain lessened. What unfolded, as I suspected might have been the case, was intense turmoil and an extreme reaction to an unusual situation the night before, when we had allowed Hayden to use the computer. He had not been allowed any computer time for over a year, for complicated reasons that are a part of his story; but on this occasion, we'd felt that we'd had to allow it.

In Genevieve's eyes and *in* her body, she experienced Hayden's use of our computer as having invaded her space and her lifeline; the result was her intense toothache. It was a heart-wrenching reminder of the traumatic connections she still harbored around him. She couldn't even sit in her old familiar computer chair without putting a blanket over it, to remove "traces of him". We undid the damage: we gave her a new, untainted chair; we assured her that it was a one-time situation and that he would not be on the computer again. She and I did a lot of soul searching and followed it up with a cleansing process through visualization and guided imagery. Her toothache magically disappeared. It was a horrible situation, but it was an amazing opportunity to show her how emotional pain and a terrible feeling of physical upheaval and invasion could be transferred into physical pain. I had seen it happen many times in her life but never to that severity. It reminded me of the group of autistic adults I'd met with years before, who had described emotional pain that affected them so deeply on a physical level, that they literally wanted to reach inside their head, or whatever part of their body where they felt it, and pull it out.

The intense toothache did go away and there was not a trace of any teeth issues until six months later. Then again, seemingly out of the blue, she was screaming and writhing in pain, tormented by another severe toothache. Suspecting a similar pattern, she and I again dissected the day and the days prior. Sure enough, another computer upheaval glared back at us. This time, our computer had not only crashed and was in for repair, but much of her cherished data had been lost. To heighten the trauma, it had happened over Thanksgiving weekend which was of course, a socially bombarding time for her. After hours of therapeutic work and visualizations, as well as the repair of our computer and the restoration of her programs and data, the toothache once again, mysteriously disappeared.

Thinking our computer-induced toothache traumas were behind us, we waited anxiously for the arrival of Genevieve's laptop, which we had been blessed to get funding for. But to our surprise, another toothache trauma awaited us. This one was even more fascinating, though more exasperating than the others.

Knowing that when her laptop arrived, she would be keeping it in her bedroom and we would no longer need the huge computer desk in my home office, we unwisely jumped the gun and did not wait until her laptop arrived, before reconfiguring our computer onto a smaller desk. The result was that it changed the *feel* of the room too dramatically for her and it also meant that she had to type with the keyboard on her lap. At the time, it didn't seem like that big of an issue, as it was only for a week or two before her laptop would arrive; and I'd hoped she would see it as part of the "adventure". I was dead wrong. Back came the intense toothache, more writhing in pain and a tormented, exasperated and confused Genevieve.

She blamed her teeth and questioned the possibility of cavities. By now the pattern was so obvious to me, but she was in such distress, she couldn't make the connection. Again, we turned to visualizations, guided imagery, soul searching, journal writing and drawing. The answer once again glared back at us: emotional pain and the intense feeling of upheaval had translated into physical pain. In response we added another temporary desk so that the keyboard was no longer on her lap. The toothache definitely improved, but only marginally.

Back to the drawing board she and I went. This time, I drew a picture of the computer the way it was on the old desk, with attention to details, even the pictures on the wall behind it. By this point, I was desperate and feeling terrible guilt at what I had inadvertently inflicted on her. I wanted her to *feel* and *see* the computer set up as it had been before. It worked and even my inadequate drawing was enough that I could see her body language change. She and I realized that what we hadn't addressed with the interim desk was the actual *angle* of the keyboard. On our original desk, the keyboard had to be on a rather awkward angle but that was the angle she was used to. That was what had to be duplicated, practically to the millimeter.

Once we did that the improvement was phenomenal but still, the toothache continued. It was now more of a dull but disconcerting throb. We were so close! Then I remembered a technique a therapist had taught me which I adapted for Genevieve. I taught her to envision white light entering the top of her head and warmly filling up every inch of her body. She and I focused on that soothing and inspirational light swishing through her mouth, encircling each tooth and around her jaws. Immediately, she found enormous relief, not complete, but close.

We made a little sign by the computer which simply said: "Breathe in white light". Over the course of the next day, she described to me how the moment she felt the dull throb returning to her mouth, she read the note, breathed in white light, swished it around her jaws and her gums and the pain went away. It was an impressive technique, as was her diligence and willingness to embrace it. This was a tough and dramatic lesson but she learned profoundly about the relationship between her body and her emotions; and we all learned that we had the power to address them!

She's had a couple more toothaches since then, not directly linked to the computer or her laptop as these had been, but certainly linked to upheavals or alterations in her personal space or environment. There have, at times, been other physical manifestations that we have recognized and explored, like the sensation of "screws being twisted into her back" when she is discussing issues that are uncomfortable to her. Sometimes they serve as a "barometer" to pinpoint underlying difficulties that she may not even be outwardly aware of.

These reactions are very intense and very complex. They take a toll on her physically and emotionally, as they do for those of us, like Madeleine and myself, who work to get her through them and to address them. But at the same time, there is almost an "honesty" in them that I have learned tremendously from. *All of us*, autistic or not, store things in our bodies! We react to things, we suppress things, we let them work their way through our bodies, sometimes affecting us in ways that we are not even aware of. I wish, because I love her so deeply, that she didn't have to deal with the intensity of these reactions; but how do I not be in awe of her for how she manages to get through them and to endure, address and learn from them? How do I not be grateful for what she has inadvertently taught me about bodies and emotions and all of that?

I do mean it from my heart when I say that for all that I have been able to teach her, it is a fraction of what she has taught me.

Chapter 35

The world of Musical Theatre and Drama *was* Genevieve's high school world. She could loose herself and expand herself and connect deeply with her peers. She told me she loved being able to present the different sides of her personality, through different roles. I sensed part of the magic lay in the fact that she could experience herself interacting with others in a way that was relatively safe and predictable, yet meaningful. Dialogue and emotions were controlled through scripts, so she could handle the social input. Her roles were a way of "taking herself off the shelf" and exploring and presenting herself, much as she did when she was younger and perused through the short tale of "Effervescence".

Though Genevieve still had to deal with the unpredictability of peer responses and the real-life drama that abounded amongst her theatre classmates, she was in her comfort zone and her abilities were all the more heightened. She made tremendous gains, socially and emotionally. She had a natural ability to memorize scripts and "feel" her role. One of her self-chosen monologues would lead to an amazing pinnacle in her life. And it would lead to the moment when I knew I could finally finish the book that I had begun writing years before. It gave me my ending.

It all started in grade twelve when her drama teacher gave her a long list of suggested monologues for an upcoming performance. Genevieve pushed them all aside and firmly insisted that there was one and only one piece that she would consider presenting, and that it meant the world to her. It was a segment from Mark Haddon's book *The Curious Incident of the Dog in the Night-Time,* which is a captivating piece of fiction that convincingly gives the feel of being narrated by a young man with autism, who was wrongly accused of killing a neighbor's dog.

Genevieve's monologue was eight minutes long, longer than any of the others; but on the night of her performance, she had her audience spellbound. I don't think she knew, because I didn't have the heart to tell her (though she will know when she reads this book), that I didn't actually make it to the theatre in time to take my place in the audience. I got held up and arrived just seconds after she began. I could have slipped in but I didn't want to risk breaking her concentration or taking any of the focus away from her. I stood at the door and listened.

There was a tiny slit, barely wide enough for me to see her shadow as she walked back and forth across the stage. To be honest, I was grateful to have had that door between us. I would have been lost in emotion, no more than a blubbering fool had I been inside, able to see her under the stage lights, watching her stirring performance. Even from my place at the door, I could feel the intensity of not only her performance, but of the audience who received it. They had been told that the monologue was taken from a book written through the eyes of a character with autism; but few knew that it was performed *by* a young woman with autism. But they could hear the conviction in her voice and they could feel the depth with which she presented her monologue; it permeated through them and there was not a sound to be heard but her voice and the beating of their enriched hearts.

Nolan and I were moved beyond words and filled with indescribable pride and awe by her performance. But what screamed from within me was: "She wants to tell! She wants people to know who she really is!" I could see it and feel it, that she was ready to take that step.

For weeks after, I carefully tiptoed around the possibility that maybe there was some hidden reason in her choosing that particular piece; but

Genevieve seemed oblivious. To her, the monologue was important to perform but it didn't seem to go beyond that, like she hadn't made the connection. I felt disappointed, like the cards were all laid out, ready and waiting to be "read"; but I had to respect her lack of inclination. So with "my tail between my legs", I admitted to myself that maybe I was wrong. Maybe her compulsion to perform that piece was simply to enlighten her audience about autism in general. The reality was that she had worked so hard throughout her high school years to cover up the fact that she had autism; maybe I was wrong then and had been all the years before, about trying to be open about it. My heart was in a suspended state of agony, teetering between the feeling of "having done wrong" and the feeling that we were so close to fruition, on what had been a driving force for so many years. Maybe I *had* been wrong! Maybe I hadn't had the right.

I secretly agonized about the two opposing predicaments and was very, very shaken up by them, to my core. Then, a few weeks later when I picked Genevieve up from school, she was in tears and visibly distraught. At first I assumed she'd had another rough day over school stress or assignments or the usual list of issues that we had been working on all year; but this felt different. She was overwrought by emotion and looked genuinely confused. Shaking her head, she whimpered: "I don't get it. In Musical Theatre there's a song that every time we sing, I fall apart".

I asked her what the song was about and she replied something about the Jews in Israel. As her Musical Theatre trip to Cuba was, at that point, just a few weeks away, I suspected that perhaps her concerns about world peace were heightened by the political unrest in Cuba, which seemed a reasonable concern. But the next day, she was still shaken; and luckily it was an art therapy day. She and Madeleine dissected the song, word for word, and deciphered the exact theme to be that of the Jews having to hide from who they really were. Upon this revelation, she apparently stopped and blurted out to Madeleine: "Oh my God, I think I need to tell everyone who I am. I have to come out!"

Later that night, when she relayed her epiphany to me, I had to contain my disbelief and gratitude that suddenly, this milestone was indeed upon us! She and I soul searched together, taking in all that she and Madeleine had surmised, to see what the next step needed to be. She was driven to act on her revelation and I was equally driven to take her lead and go wherever it seemed meant to go. Together, we composed a letter. It was simple, not belabored or grammatically flawless; but it was from her heart and that made it perfect. There was no right or wrong or anything that could be challenged because this was the real thing: this was *her* life put into a few, beautifully composed paragraphs! It was a fascinating process of guiding her into understanding her feelings and channeling them into that letter, all of it coming so deep from within her. The moment we wrote the final word, I saw in her an immediate sense of peace, of resolution and even excitement! She felt compelled to read it to the classmates that meant the most to her, her Musical Theatre class.

Madeleine and I could not have been more proud of her or more thrilled. This was what she and I had been working on for years. No matter what the consequences, *it was time.* We both could feel it! The next day I contacted Genevieve's teachers to prepare them, so that they could support her if necessary, and be ready to address any fallout that might be the result amongst her or the class when she presented it. They were of course, wonderfully supportive and no doubt, in awe of her bravery. She was nervous, not knowing if she would be able to hold it together well enough to read her letter, and not knowing how the others would respond. For support, she reached out bravely the Saturday night before the determined date, by emailing one of the more sensitive girls from her class. She disclosed her plan, included her letter for the girl to read and asked that when the time came, if she faltered or lacked the courage to continue, that this girl step in and finish for her.

This lovely girl was a good choice. She was genuinely moved not only by Genevieve's letter and her bravery, but by being the one who was chosen.

A couple of days later the stage was set; the support systems were in place and Genevieve was filled with nervous conviction. With bated breath, fingers crossed and Madeleine and all of Genevieve's family "waiting in the wings" to hear how it all went down, she and I drove off to school. Today was the day. But on the short drive to school, my cell phone rang and on the other end was Mr. Gripp, from the Learning Assistance department. Knowing what was about to transpire, he knew he had to intersect and pass on that this was *not* the day for her revelation; this was in fact, the worst possible day. The school had just received notice that Mr. Montage, the beloved Musical Theatre director, had passed away.

Though Mr. Montage had been away on medical leave for many months, none of the students were expecting this news. Genevieve was devastated and heart broken, as was the entire school community and our community around it. Even I had been blessed by my interactions with this amazing, larger than life man and had received my fair share of the infamous Mr. Montage hugs; but I felt another loss resulting. I felt his loss but also the loss of what was supposed to be a vital turning point in one of his student's life. This event, her "Coming Out" as we called it, would have filled him with immeasurable pride and wonder. What would he have said, how would he have felt if he knew that the momentum had been lost, perhaps never to find the right time or the right dynamics again? He would have wrapped his arms around Genevieve, kissed her wild, red hair and told her to do what he taught everyone he came in contact with to do: to love herself and dare to be who she was. He would have told her to get on with it and not let anything get in her way!

Time was of the essence, especially with the trip to Cuba just weeks away and grade-twelve graduation just beyond that. Both Madeleine and I felt certain that Genevieve's "coming out letter" was an unexpected "key", a key that would help to unlock not just a single but a two-sided door. One door would enable her to feel more accepted and more at peace; the second door would offer her peers answers to some of their questions and observations of Genevieve. That, we were certain, would translate into even greater support and understanding. With respect to Cuba, we had support systems in place, but Cuba was a long distance away with many possibilities for issues, and we were mortified. We knew that it was imperative that our main support system stem from her classmates themselves, and their level of acceptance and tolerance. This letter *was* a key. Mr. Montage would have seen it the same way; we were certain of it.

That day had not been the right day; the following day was not the right day. Everyone, including Genevieve was in mourning. But the third day just seemed to fit. It was a way of not loosing momentum but refueling with momentum, because it was in fact, a way of honoring Mr. Montage and what he stood for. I think it actually helped the Musical Theatre department deal with their loss. And so, through a few, brief lines added to the beginning of her letter, Genevieve explained why she felt that this sad time in each of their lives was also an appropriate time, to do what she was about to do.

And she did do it! She read her letter. After school, she described the event in detail. She told us how her teachers had briefly explained to the class that she had something important to share with them. She described how, as she walked up to the front of her class, three people patted her on the leg and urged her on. She read the whole letter on her own. She admitted it was hard, that she had been shaking and that at some points she cried. But she did it!

After her final words, her class clapped and someone called out: "We love you Genevieve!" There were lots of comments, beautiful ones. The entire class joined hands and formed a "cinnamon bun", with Genevieve tightly rolled up in the center.

At home that evening, we set out candles and crystal wine glasses. We celebrated with gifts of pink roses and starry rhinestones. We toasted Genevieve for her courage and for being the amazing inspiration that she was!

With Genevieve's permission, her "Coming Out" words are here for you to hear as well:

> *"That song in Musical Theatre got me on such a strong emotional level and it made me question "Why? What was in it that touched me so deeply?" So I sat down and thought about the words, the history and the Jewish community having to hide who they were. It made me realize that for the past five years, I had been hiding who I am from so many people.*
>
> *What I've been hiding is something that is part of who I am. Some of you may remember how important it was for me to perform my monologue from the book "The Curious Incident of the Dog in the Night-Time". It's a story about a teenager who has autism, which is something I have.*
>
> *There is a huge range of how autism can affect a person. I want to explain how it applies to me...*
>
> *I have had so many challenges to deal with in my life but it has also given me many gifts. It's part of what has made me who I am.*
>
> *Having autism has given me a whole lot of perspective on people and everyday situations. Someone with autism processes information differently than an average person would. Autism also affects the sensory system so that things can appear, sound, feel and taste differently to me than they would for others.*
>
> *For these reasons, I do see the world very differently. I've experienced things on a very different level. Sometimes it can be hard to relate to other people but if I do find someone I can connect and identify with, we are able to look at the world from a very unique perspective.*
>
> *That is why writing, drawing, acting, music and singing mean so much to me. They allow me to take on other perspectives. It's fun, interesting and liberating.*

With having autism, every good thing comes with a price to pay. I get overwhelmed by certain situations such as social situations. I don't know what to say or do. That's one of the biggest challenges of autism. In fact, it is at the heart of autism. It's hard to "be on" all the time, to be talkative and social all the time. There are times when I need to step away from everything and take some time for myself. Whether it's at school, at home or wherever, that's just the way it is.

Verbally, I have trouble getting my point across, but when I pick up a pen or sit at a computer, it comes naturally. It flows out of me like a waterfall.

Math and Science have always been hard for me and people seem to affiliate being skilled at Math is a measure of intelligence. I feel that the fact that I go to the LA Center gives people the impression that I'm inadequate without realizing that for me, having autism isn't a question of intellect, it's a matter of needing space and a time to process.

One of the things I love about this class is that we seem to love and accept each other. We're free to be who we are. We've seen each other's ups and downs; we've seen each other wear almost next to nothing; we've laughed at each other's jokes, and we've applauded each other's talents.

This feels like the right time in my life and I feel you guys are the ones I feel safest telling all of this to. I want to thank you for hearing me out and taking time to stick through all of this".

As I said earlier, her letter was "simple, not belabored or grammatically flawless but from her heart and that made it perfect. There was no right or wrong or anything that could be challenged because this was the real thing: this was her life put in a few beautifully-composed paragraphs".

Chapter 36

On a personal level, I can hardly describe how validating Genevieve's "Coming Out" experience had been. For the four years leading up to it, I'd watched her and had been aware how hard she had worked to hide her autism. I'd agonized over the feeling that maybe I had been wrong all those years in preschool and elementary school, for being open about what autism was and that she had it. Maybe I really hadn't had that right.

But the concept of covering up was so foreign to me. Our journey had never been an easy one and there had been battles; but I had always felt in my heart, that there was only one direction to move. Throughout high school, I'd had to bite my lip and honor Genevieve's choice because it was, after all, her life not mine. It was her decision; but it had never felt right to me to try to hide the fact that she had autism. Would I have tried to hide the fact if she was, for example, deaf or blind or diabetic? No; of course not. I'd *never* seen it as "labeling" her; I saw it as acceptance. And I saw it as having faith in the world around her.

That was why I had fought so hard for so many years, to not follow simply the traditional approaches. Some worked for Genevieve, many did not. And in my eyes, it was never all about "behavior modification". It was about bits of behavior modification and lots of enabling a child to accept who she was, to accept some degree of her limitations but to embrace what made her unique, and to then build onto that uniqueness in every avenue of her life.

I knew there were times when even Dr. Bryson was intrigued by our approaches and he sometimes questioned them; but always, he saw the results and he recognized and celebrated them. He too, fought back tears of joy, disbelief and immeasurable pride as he read paragraph after paragraph of Genevieve's amazing "coming out" letter. And he too, saw it as confirmation and validation of the path, with all of its twists and turns, that we had chosen. Like me, he probably also let out a breath of relief, to see that validation, and to acknowledge her emergence and the remarkable young woman she had become. I'm sure there were times over the years when he questioned our path, probably more than he let on. Many times I did challenge him to look outside of his comfort zone; but equally there were times when he had to skillfully and carefully find ways to harness and guide me. We were impressive partners, as we remain today.

Without Dr. Bryson's input, his unique insight and experience and the countless hours that he dedicated to us, many chapters of this tale would have been profoundly different, much less the ending. He understood who we were as a family, and more than that, who I was and who Genevieve was and what we were capable of. At times when I was filled with self doubt about my own abilities and my strength to forge on, he empowered me, time and time again. When Genevieve made the transition into junior high school, he wrote a letter to staff in complete support of the path that as a family, we had chosen to follow and of the skills he saw in me. He has been very forthright in saying that he has learned a great deal from us over the years. These are his words:

> "The last decade has been a pivotal one in the treatment of autism. Although we have always known about rare cases of children with autism recovering "spontaneously", recent advances have assisted more and more children to function in normal or near normal ways. The ingredients needed to facilitate these "good outcomes" are just now being identified. Genevieve was fortunate to be born in a family of supportive, gifted, energetic people who were quick to identify her differences, resourceful in

finding ways to truly understand her, and relentless in creating opportunities for her to learn and grow. Simone in particular, has an uncanny ability to see life through Genevieve's eyes, to anticipate problems and successes, and to translate the world for Genevieve and, as in "Effervescence" (the original, abbreviated tale), translate Genevieve to the world.

Whereas most interventions for autistic children involve directly suppressing autistic behaviors and training competing skills, the Brennemans have been able to achieve excellent progress for Genevieve by working *with* Genevieve's autistic features and obsessions and gently channeling them into knowledge and skills that have facilitated her development. They have also helped Genevieve to develop some of the talents that enrich her life and *draw others to her*. I am always impressed when children with autism function as well as Genevieve by her age. I am doubly impressed when the route to this good outcome was forged by a family following their own path, relying on their own intuitions, and creating their own successes. Genevieve is a remarkable, delightful young lady and her family, both parents and siblings, are equally remarkable".

It would be naïve to say that Genevieve's "coming out" letter meant that she had come to complete terms with having autism. But it was an important step in her having faith in herself, and her capacity to be recognized, loved and admired for who she was. And it was an important step in her having faith in the people she *chose* to tell. It was a turning point in her life and it was something to celebrate. This was an intensely personal experience for her, which she has allowed me to share, though anonymously. She has come to recognize that she truly is an incredible inspiration and she can help to change the lives of other people who share the common threads of autism. She can help to open the world's eyes and understand that autism is *"not a terrible disease that should be cured!"* Those are *her* words.

Chapter 37

Often when I watch Genevieve, I'm happy to see that she still has her effervescence, that image that her feet never quite touch the ground. I see it when she flits from one activity or one room to another, smiling to herself. It's so unique; typically people don't smile unless they're smiling at someone or unless they are really excited about whatever that next activity is going to be. It's not the same thing. I see her smile and it is a smile that comes from her heart, meant only for her. It's beautiful.

When she first gets up in the morning she floats, though predictably, the long way around through the kitchen and into the dining room because for some reason, that's the path she takes. Her head is still slightly turned, so that she's not looking directly at any of us. Perhaps she's savoring the last moments of her private world before she enters ours'. She's not a tiny or particularly graceful person and yet she wafts in, glides into her chair and folds her hands together in front of her lap. It's just so unique and when we are drawn to impersonate her subtle entrance, she loves it and laughs. To us it's like: "Look what the wind blew in!"

Likewise, when she's had enough of us, she picks herself up and floats away. Sometimes, I think if we blinked twice, we wouldn't have even seen, felt or heard her leave. By contrast, if two of us are sitting on the couch and she has decided it's a time that she wants to share with us, she may float in and then literally wedge herself into the three inches that were between us (personal space, too much or not enough, are still interesting issues). She is a unique soul!

The months that followed Genevieve's "Coming Out" were the most socially-successful months of her life. Her Musical Theatre trip to Cuba was overall, a success and she had a great time. There's *no* doubt that her openness and honesty about who she was, did open up a two-way door. For her, she felt more at peace with herself and in turn, acted more naturally around her peers and friends. For them, her little "quirks" and episodes where she did need their support and understanding, then made sense. They were able to respond with greater respect and genuine caring. (To slip ahead because you are probably wondering and hoping: at the time of publication of this book: some of the members of this magical Musical Theatre group have continued their connection beyond graduation and Genevieve remains a welcomed part of that).

The timing of Genevieve's "Coming Out" just three months prior to her graduation, was truly amazing. The image that hit us each, her family, her therapists and her teachers, so deeply, was the thought of her walking down the runway at her valedictory ceremony, genuinely being who she really was, and being proud of all that she had accomplished! That gave each of us the patience and conviction we needed to help her overcome all of the pre-grad obstacles and emotional ups and downs that lay ahead.

Chapter 38

Genevieve did graduate. She went to her graduation banquet and had a fabulous time! Unlike most of the other young women who looked breath-taking but rather predictable in their rainbow array of "poofy" prom dresses, she wore an authentic, medieval gown in dark forest green. It had been designed and intricately hand-made by a most unique and creative seamstress, whose spirit and mannerisms held an uncanny resemblance to Genevieve.

The adventure of "acquiring" Genevieve's graduation dress remains one of my most personal and beautiful, though complex, experiences with Genevieve. It ended up not being simply a teen in search of a prom dress; it was a remarkable process of self discovery, a tale all of its own. It was on my birthday and if only for that reason, it will remain a tale whose fascinating details I want to keep to myself.

With her long red hair and vibrant medieval gown, Genevieve was captivating and unique! It was beautifully ironic that this girl who, not so many years before, would spin in circles dressed in poofy princess dresses, and who would have been devastated to her core had she been forced to wear something else, would toss aside her pink poofiness for the event of "her ball". Instead, she wrapped herself up in "history, truth, honesty, graceful swans, forests and unique beauty". Those were the words she told me she felt when she slipped into her dress.

But true to her beloved Cinderella, a horse-drawn carriage was exactly how our heroine arrived at her graduation ball. As a family (less Hayden), we rode together through the lush park that runs through our city, then through the busy downtown streets of rush-hour and up to the steps that led to her destination: High School Graduation.

Chapter 39

*T*he Valedictory Ceremony, the official mark of graduation, was of no less intensity and emotion! As we bustled with the final details of the hair, the make-up and the traditional, black graduation gown, there was a knock at our door. To our absolute astonishment and delight, stood Genevieve's kindergarten teacher, her grade seven teacher and her beloved elementary special ed assistant. They had roses and hugs and were bursting with pride and excitement! Genevieve was moved beyond words and I thought my heart would burst. These three women were such an important part of our journey and of our history. To have them there at that moment, on that day, was a testament to their dedication *and* to the profound impact that Genevieve had had on their lives. To see their arms wrapped around her and then wrapped around me, made all those years melt away, and it was just us, co-conspirators in Genevieve's on-going tale. There are many, many people who have been a part of this tale!

A short while later, Nolan and I watched Genevieve during her Valedictory Ceremony. She looked beautiful, taking it all in. She was calm, but excited and glowing, everything a young woman at her graduation should be. It was quite a different picture from the wild little munchkin who spun in circles at her baby brother's baptism, or the tormented child lying on her back screaming, alongside her brother, who was also screaming and spinning in his own circles, years before.

That's not to say that all the challenges are behind her. Every single day will have its challenges and often there are still meltdowns. There remain mountains that at times feel insurmountable. But on *that* day, despite the hundreds of excited souls nestled around her, she was radiant in her pride for all that she had accomplished and the new route her life was taking. Even the surprise announcement of her name, the winner of a special scholarship for the "student with the greatest tenacity in her studies" was not enough to throw her. She only responded with all the more pride, as she walked gracefully to receive it.

The thunderous applause, on that occasion, filled her body and her soul with joy, not anxiety or the need to make them all go away. My only regret in sharing that moment with hundreds upon hundreds of cheering graduates and their families, was that she couldn't hear Nolan, Kobe, Sydney and myself, or see how proud we were of her. But I think she knew.

Genevieve was effervescence and courage all wrapped up in one!

As I write the last line of this tale, my part is done. I hope that someday a sequel will be written, but that it will be written by our heroine herself. Then it would be a tale right from the "horse's mouth", or in this case, the pink and black zebra-striped horse's mouth! I asked Genevieve awhile back, if she ever thinks about writing her amazing story, her unique autobiography. After barely a moment, she replied: "Yeah, maybe. But right now, I've got way too many ideas for plays kickin' around in my head!"

We're ready and waiting for those too!

The End

Footnotes

1. Williams, Donna. *Nobody Nowhere*. (Doubleday Canada Limited, Toronto, 1992), page xv.

2. Grandin, Temple and Margaret M. Scariano. *Emergence: Labeled Autistic*. (Warner Books Inc., New York, 1986), page 82

3. Williams, Donna. *Nobody Nowhere*. (Doubleday Canada Limited, Toronto, 1992), page 5.

The Castle We Called Home

Simone Brenneman

"When our son Hayden reached the turning point of moving from elementary school to junior high, I knew it was the time to repeat the process I had been so compelled to follow a few years earlier with Genevieve. But in picking up a pen, I could feel that this story, and the process itself, would be very different from hers'. I wouldn't be able to put Hayden in the leading role as simply as I had done with Genevieve in *Effervescence*. And this wouldn't be a tale; it would be an epic. It wouldn't be light and pink and fluffy, with twists and turns, as her story had been. It *would* be an epic journey of a complex, brooding force that prevailed and altered all of those around it.

Even as I began to write the first few sentences, I could feel the familiar stone walls going up around me, and around the five people that I loved. I could feel the turmoil that existed from within the walls, as well as from beyond. In our home, it often felt like the world was pushing in on us. I needed to be on guard at all times, to keep the six of us safe and thriving. This story would not be the tale of an adorable boy with wavy, red hair and the cutest dimples, who gave hugs like no one else. The reason was that the presence of Hayden in our lives had been so profound and yet so sweet, often to the point of emotional overload, that our lives had been turned upside down, inside out and contorted in ways few people could even imagine.

This story would be an "epic" about an *amazing* place, a *real* place, and *a state of mind*. It was a complex, captivating place that had weathered incredible changes and exasperating times. This epic would be about a home; it was the castle that *we* called home.

The epic would reflect our castle, which was our reality and our existence. It was where the six of us lived as individuals *and* as a family. It was strong like a fortress, often separating us from the rest of the world, sometimes because we wanted it to, and sometimes because we had no choice. Often the drawbridge was up and we kept to ourselves. Sometimes it was down, allowing us to leave. At times, we tiptoed cautiously, other times we frolicked playfully; and sometimes we ran to escape!

At this turning point in Hayden's life, I knew that anyone involved with him on any level, needed to be aware of the castle in which we lived. My story, or my epic tale as it felt that I was embarking upon, was my way of opening up the door, so that each person involved in his life could peak inside. I filled close to one hundred pages with complex and colorful bits of information and images; but it was barely enough to scratch the surface!

In published, book format, you now have the extended, fuller version and yet even that could be much longer. There are chapters upon chapters that I could have included. At this moment, I hope you are feeling just a little bit intrigued and curious enough to come inside and take a peak.

🌀🌀🌀🌀🌀🌀🌀🌀🌀🌀🌀🌀🌀🌀🌀🌀

The reality is: it's not enough to just peak inside. To know Hayden, to know us and to understand our castle, you have to come in and feel it. You need to walk around and feel each room and each person who lived there. You may at times, feel overwhelmed…how could you not? But my hope is that you will feel what I feel, which is fascination and awe. Look at the bigger picture. By stepping inside, you are becoming a part of something important and unique. Your life will be enriched in ways you will have a hard time duplicating. You will see the world through different eyes: through the eyes of our two children challenged by autism, and through the eyes of the four of us who are blessed to have them in our lives.

Both *Effervescence* and *The Castle We Called Home,* are not only tales about autism; they are true-life tales about courage and about evolving".

About the Author

Living very much submerged in the complex worlds of her two children affected by autism, has given Simone Brenneman a unique and insightful vantage point. She is a mother of two daughters and two sons. As described in *Effervescence,* one daughter is challenged and deeply gifted, in part, by autism. One son is challenged by autism, ADHD, Cri du Chat Syndrome and a number of developmental issues, and is in his own way, gifted. Throughout her family's journey, Ms. Brenneman has acted as an integral behavior interventionist, as well as a successful home school program designer and teacher. She also has a long history of designing unique and child-specific strategies and programs for her own children.

Ms.Brenneman lives a fascinating life in British Columbia, Canada, where she daily integrates her bountiful experiences, observations and musings about the world of autism, with her other passion of working with and affecting children and adults through dance, yoga and writing.

In the past, Ms. Brenneman has worked as a special education assistant and currently works as a behavior interventionist for several beautiful children challenged by autism. Her Bachelor of Arts degree in English provides the backbone for past, present and future writing endeavors. However, the heart of her writing comes from the incredible life experiences she has been blessed to have.